Becky Thompson and Susan K. Pitts

BESTSELLING AUTHORS

tonight we pray
for the momma

100 Midnight Mom Devotions and Prayers

TYNDALE
MOMENTUM®

A Tyndale nonfiction imprint

Visit Tyndale online at tyndale.com.

Visit Becky and Susan at midnightmomdevotional.com.

Tyndale, Tyndale's quill logo, *Tyndale Momentum*, and the Tyndale Momentum logo are registered trademarks of Tyndale House Ministries. Tyndale Momentum is a nonfiction imprint of Tyndale House Publishers, Carol Stream, Illinois.

Tonight We Pray for the Momma: 100 Midnight Mom Devotions and Prayers

Copyright © 2023 by Thompson Family Ministries LLC and Susan K. Pitts. All rights reserved.

Cover and interior illustration of house copyright © Torico/Shutterstock. All rights reserved.

Cover and interior illustration of stars copyright © George Peters/Getty Images. All rights reserved.

Author photograph provided by authors; used with permission. All rights reserved.

Cover designed by Dean H. Renninger

The authors are represented by Alive Literary Agency, www.aliveliterary.com.

All Scripture quotations, unless otherwise indicated, are taken from the Holy Bible, *New International Version,*® *NIV.*® Copyright © 1973, 1978, 1984, 2011 by Biblica, Inc.® Used by permission. All rights reserved worldwide.

Scripture quotations marked BSB are taken from The Holy Bible, Berean Study Bible, BSB. Copyright © 2016, 2018 by Bible Hub. Used by permission. All rights reserved worldwide.

Scripture quotations marked CSB are taken from the Christian Standard Bible,® copyright © 2017 by Holman Bible Publishers. Used by permission. Christian Standard Bible® and CSB® are federally registered trademarks of Holman Bible Publishers.

Scripture quotations marked ERV are taken from the *Holy Bible*, Easy-to-Read Version, copyright © 2013, 2016 by Bible League International. Used by permission. All rights reserved.

All Scripture quotations marked ESV are from The ESV® Bible (The Holy Bible, English Standard Version®), copyright © 2001 by Crossway, a publishing ministry of Good News Publishers. Used by permission. All rights reserved.

Scripture quotations marked KJV are taken from the *Holy Bible*, King James Version.

Scripture quotations marked NKJV are taken from the New King James Version,® copyright © 1982 by Thomas Nelson. Used by permission. All rights reserved.

Scripture quotations marked NLT are taken from the *Holy Bible*, New Living Translation, copyright © 1996, 2004, 2015 by Tyndale House Foundation. Used by permission of Tyndale House Publishers, Carol Stream, Illinois 60188. All rights reserved.

For information about special discounts for bulk purchases, please contact Tyndale House Publishers at csresponse@tyndale.com, or call 1-855-277-9400.

Library of Congress Cataloging-in-Publication Data

A catalog record for this book is available from the Library of Congress.

ISBN 978-1-4964-8270-9

Printed in China

29	28	27	26	25	24	23
7	6	5	4	3	2	1

To all our midnight mommas who show up and pray with us nightly . . .
this book is for you. May the Lord meet you on each page.

to you, momma,
before we begin

BEFORE YOU EVEN KNEW THIS BOOK EXISTED, we prayed for you. We prayed for the momma who often walks the line between joy and sorrow, hope and heartache, anxiety and peace. We prayed for the momma who loves her children but is tired. She's grateful for the family God has given her, but she has so many questions in her heart and so many feelings about the painful places on the path she has walked. She turns to God for help, hope, and healing, and still most days she feels a little bit of everything. Even though she juggles so many plates, there's often one thing so heavy on her heart.

She may feel anxious, overwhelmed, or exhausted to her core. Some days she doesn't even know what she feels. But despite her own stress, she leans into God for strength, peace, and guidance. She asks Him to help her make the right decisions and to reassure her that she is doing a good job. Some days she feels as if she is barely making it, but she keeps putting one foot in front of the other.

Her children may be of any age. There are so many reasons moms often see midnight. She might be the momma running her kids to and from appointments and activities, burning her candle at both ends as the events of the day stretch well into the night. She might be the momma of a newborn. She might be an empty nester, reaching across town or across the country with both active love and unceasing prayer, awake at all hours. She may be the stepmom, foster mom, bonus mom, aunt, or nana. Whether her kids are hers by birth or by choice, she loves the family God designed just for her.

It's for this momma—for you—that we have been praying nightly since 2015, and it's you we had in mind as we wrote these prayers and devotions.

When you imagine the place where we wrote this letter to you, you might picture a table in a kitchen, dining room, or perhaps a local coffee shop (though our town is too small for one of those). In fact, our worktable was pulled from the backyard after it didn't sell on Facebook Marketplace. After wiping it clean of cobwebs and the red Oklahoma dirt, we placed it next to the window seat in Momma's bedroom where the sunniest of light pours through the tree branches outside.

This was a quiet place for important conversations. It was where we told our stories and read God's Word, one of us sometimes slipping a round butterscotch candy to the other when the writing got hard. It was where we found encouragement and hope, not just for the sweet things in life, but for the heavy things as well. Sometimes as we recounted the ways God had met us in our journeys, the tears outweighed the laughter.

The truth is, this book of devotions isn't just for the lighter moments of motherhood. This book is for you, Momma, in all of your midnight moments.

Who are we? We are a mother (Susan) and daughter (Becky) who didn't set out to lead almost two million praying moms online, but that's what we do today. All across social media, you'll see our prayers, each of which begins with these seven familiar words: "Tonight we pray for the momma who . . ."

The Lord is our ultimate hope, and we cling to Him for strength during all the hard moments of motherhood. We recognize there are so many. Yes, there are happy times full of joy when we celebrate and rejoice in God's goodness. But in this book, we believe God asked us to point to all the places in our stories where He meets us when the light seems dim, we can't see His presence, and we need Him to bring healing in places of heartache.

Tonight We Pray for the Momma reaches into so many areas of a momma's heart and offers you an opportunity to meet with the Lord who heals, restores, and brings you hope, even in your weariest moments. You may recognize some of the prayers in this book from one of our viral posts. We gathered one hundred of our most beloved and widely shared prayers from the thousands we have written and posted online. We then paired each one with stories of hope and encouragement from our lives and the Word of God. That's what you'll find in the pages ahead.

Each of these devotions is truly a colabor of love, written by both of us. When a story begins from one of our perspectives, you will surely be able to tell from context who is initially speaking— only one of us is a grandmother!—but the heartbeat of each day comes from both mother and daughter.

Read one devotional at a time, or as many as you need each night. Open the book to see what the next page says or turn to the back and search through the index to find hope in the midst of whatever you face. We invite you to make each prayer your own by engaging with the simple prompt that follows each one. You can decide whether to whisper or write your response.

Momma, this book was written just for you. It's our honor to walk with you through these one hundred midnight mom devotions and prayers.

Tonight we pray for the momma *who holds this book in her hands. Lord, You know her full story and right where she stands today. You see every need, every area that needs healing. You hear every question she hasn't even asked. Lead her deeper into Your love and meet her through the pages ahead. Please give her rest tonight. We ask in Jesus's name, amen.*

So much love,
Becky and Susan

who has one thing so heavy on her heart

Cast your burden on the Lord, *and he will sustain you;*
he will never allow the righteous to be shaken.

PSALM 55:22, csb

One day I was in the kitchen refilling my glass of water when my eleven-year-old daughter walked in the house and asked if she could watch a show in the living room. Distracted, I agreed and turned back toward my office. We were in the process of yet another move, and it had been a hectic few weeks. Working from home was harder than usual. With clutter and boxes and a life that wasn't fully in one location or another, everything seemed anything but settled. No matter what else I needed to do or think about, details surrounding the move played like a background track in my mind.

Twenty minutes later, unable to focus, I walked back out of my office again. That's when I noticed my daughter in the big, comfortable chair in our living room. After removing her shoes, she had collapsed into her favorite spot and hunched forward. She was completely oblivious to the fact that she hadn't removed her backpack when she sat down to rest. I chuckled and wondered how she had been able to ignore the heavy pack—until I realized that what I saw reflected my own situation.

How many times had I prayed even that day, "Lord, help me with this move. It feels like too much. I'm overwhelmed and stressed, and I can't get it all done"? How many times, both through Scripture and whispers directly to my heart, had God told me, *Give it to Me. I'll carry it, and I'll carry you. Cast your burden on Me, and I will sustain you?* And how many times had I been so focused on my need for rest that I hadn't practiced the simple and yet imperative task of taking off what I needed to set down?

I just wanted peace, stability, and the reassurance that everything was going to turn out okay. I'm no stranger to these heart needs. I think if we're honest with our own feelings, this is what all mommas crave, no matter what we face.

We want to know that the one issue that weighs heaviest on our hearts and minds has an answer and resolution. We want to know that God sees us *and our needs.* More than that, we want to know that He cares and will help us with all we've been shouldering.

Momma, God never intended for you to bear the weight of unanswered questions or cumbersome concerns on your own.

The truth is, you might not know the answers, but He does. You might not have your own peace, but He gives you His. He has all that you need, and you have Him. Tonight let's make an exchange. Let's cast our burdens on Him and receive the reassurance that He doesn't just know what we need—He will also carry us through.

Tonight we pray for the momma *with one thing so heavy on her heart. Lord, we don't know what it is she's facing, but You do. You know all sides of the situation. You are with this momma as she thinks it over and wonders and worries. And in the middle of it all, You hold her close and tell her again and again, "I've got it. You're okay. It's going to be okay. I have it." Help her to feel You and hear You tonight. You're louder than the fear, closer than she realizes, and fully able to take care of what needs to be done. Help her place this one thing into Your capable hands. Help her step out of the worry tonight.*

We ask in Jesus's name, amen.

Lord, these things are so heavy
on my heart right now:

who feels a little bit of everything

Every good and perfect gift is from above,
coming down from the Father of the heavenly lights,
who does not change like shifting shadows.

JAMES 1:17

I'VE BEEN A MOMMA FOR FOUR DECADES NOW, but when I had my first baby, I was so nervous that I was going to make a mistake. My extended family—my own momma, aunts, and cousins—lived far away, and I very much felt the absence of that generational support. I remember that in those early days I felt a little bit of everything. Weariness, joy, and loneliness seemed to happen all at once, especially late at night when the house was quiet and the voices of discouragement and fear seemed to be the loudest.

I picked up a valuable lesson in those midnight hours that has kept me in good stead all my years as a momma. I learned the power of praying and asking the Lord into my situation. As the rocking chair would go *click, click, click*, I would bring each prayer request to Him. It was like a midnight metronome that set the rhythm of my motherhood.

Maybe you are still in those early days of mothering, or maybe your own midnight hours are filled with memories from seasons past. In either case, when you and I feel a little bit of everything, we can trust that God has the answer we need.

Despite the changing seasons of motherhood, the Lord remains the same. Whether we feel worried or joyful, hopeful, or discouraged, at peace or overwhelmed with grief and heartache, the Lord stays steadfast and loves us through it all. He offers His presence as a gift.

Friend, I know that most of the time you're not feeling just one emotion. You're sorting through several at once. You need God's help in so many areas. The good news, as James 1:17 reminds us, is that "every good and perfect gift is from above, coming down from the Father of the heavenly lights, who does not change like shifting shadows."

The Lord is steady even when life is not. The rhythm of His heart is true and constant. He can help us navigate not only the tasks that must be done but also the tangle of our own hearts when we feel a little bit of everything.

Tonight we pray for the momma *who feels a little bit of every-thing. Lord, she may feel tired, discouraged, or worn thin. She might feel over-whelmed or sad. Hope may come in waves, or perhaps fear rests just beneath the surface of her busy mind. Lord, she is doing the best she can to sort through what needs to be done and her feelings one by one. Tonight we ask You to bring what her heart needs. If it's peace, You promise it. If it's strength, You're already there. If it's hope or joy, bubble it up from inside her. If it's rest, meet her here.*

We ask in Jesus's name, amen.

Lord, steady the rhythm of my heart
and help me sort through all of these emotions:

_____

_____

_____

_____

_____

_____

_____

_____

who didn't know
she could be this strong

*She got a basket made of papyrus reeds and waterproofed it
with tar and pitch. She put the baby in the basket and laid
it among the reeds along the bank of the Nile River.*

EXODUS 2:3, NLT

YOU MIGHT NOT RECOGNIZE the name Jochebed immediately,
but this momma in Scripture had faith that ultimately brought
freedom to her nation and her people. Jochebed was the mother
of Moses, an Israelite boy born during the time in which Pharaoh
decreed all male Hebrew children be put to death.

Pharaoh feared that the Israelites would rise against the
Egyptians, so his plan was to put an end to the next generation of
boys before they could grow into warring men. He demanded that
each male newborn be thrown into the Nile River. But the Hebrew
mother Jochebed did not fear Pharaoh. She revered God, and

when she gave birth to her third child, a baby boy, she defied the Egyptian ruler.

Jochebed hid Moses for three months until she knew she could no longer conceal him. Then, Exodus 2:3 says, "She got a basket made of papyrus reeds and waterproofed it with tar and pitch. She put the baby in the basket and laid it among the reeds along the bank of the Nile River."

Can you imagine that with me for just a moment? Jochebed, holding her newborn baby, hushing his cries, knowing day and night they could be discovered. Can you imagine her constantly swaying and rocking and holding and calming and daily trusting God to protect her and her son? Can you picture her as she carefully coated a basket, making sure no water would seep inside, because she was preparing to put her infant into this small boat? Can you see her slipping the baby from her shoulder, down into the ark, securing the ark in the reeds, and walking away? Can you imagine the cries she heard ring out loud and clear for the first time, those sobs that she had muffled for three months?

Moses was rescued from the water by Pharaoh's daughter and grew to be the man who would lead the Israelites out of Pharaoh's grip and right into the hand of God's good and merciful freedom. Moses's momma didn't just save her baby; through him, she saved the nation of Israel.

The truth is, you and I are a lot like Jochebed. We obviously face different circumstances, but we also are women willing to do whatever it takes to love, protect, and provide for our children. We are also women seeking to trust God even when we face impossible circumstances. My friend, I don't know what you're dealing with. I don't know to what extent you're placing your children into the ark of God's presence, asking Him to take care of them, but I believe that His arms will keep them afloat. His arms will strengthen yours. You might not have known you could be this strong, but God sees and knows every outcome, and you can trust Him.

Tonight we pray for the momma *who didn't know she could be this strong. Lord, she didn't know she had this in her. She didn't know she could push herself to this point. She might have thought she was strong before, but this strong? Lord, tonight we ask You to help her and remind her that she doesn't have to rely on her own strength. You are there with her. Help her rely on You. Lift off the heaviness. Hold back the fear. Blow away all the anxiety. And pull her near.*

We ask in Jesus's name, amen.

Father, please fill me
with faith and fortitude so I can . . .

who is struggling with anxiety

Do not be anxious about anything, but in every situation, by prayer and petition, with thanksgiving, present your requests to God.

PHILIPPIANS 4:6

ONE DAY IN EARLY DECEMBER, Mark and I had plans to attend a wedding at a big downtown church. A person my whole family loved would be married that day in a happy ceremony followed by a reception in the church's great hall, which was decked out with beautiful decorations. Christmas poinsettias lined the stage, and flowers adorned the room. The guests would celebrate as if it were an early Christmas party with the added joy of a loved one's wedding.

I woke up that morning so looking forward to the event. But in the back of my mind I wondered, *Can I do this? Can I go into this big crowd of people and not panic?* I wanted to go. I kept telling myself it would be all right and nothing bad would happen. I wouldn't have tunnel vision or a racing heart. I wouldn't feel the need to run out of the room or hide in the bathroom as I tried to catch my breath.

But at the last minute, just like so many other last minutes before, I came up with a reason not to attend. I was disappointed in myself because once again anxiety had kept me from doing something I really wanted to do. Like so many other times, too numerous to count, anxiety had put up a fence and hemmed me in.

Truthfully, I had suffered from anxiety since I was a child, and although I had developed coping strategies that allowed me to do many things, sometimes the big events were still just way too much.

As someone who struggles with anxiety, one passage in Philippians is particularly hard for me: "Do not be anxious about anything, but in every situation, by prayer and petition, with thanksgiving, present your requests to God." I wanted to trust God, to believe His Word, and to live it out daily. Yet I felt like a failure because I was anxious and couldn't seem to follow this instruction. But I wasn't a failure, and neither are you.

What I didn't know then was that, just like someone with a broken leg, hearing loss, or any other ailment, the anxiety I experienced was a condition that needed to be addressed through one of the many streams of healing that God uses for His glory.

Momma, the Lord knows every physical, emotional, and mental

aspect of the anxiety you are dealing with tonight. He understands how your anxiety began—whether through genetics, a traumatic event, or another cause. He is right there walking beside you each step of the way on your healing journey.

Tonight we pray for the momma *who is struggling with anxiety. Lord, she often feels overwhelmed, discouraged, afraid, or lonesome. She feels like she's just surviving. This year has already been so hard on her mental health. She keeps reminding herself that she's been through more difficult times, but she's struggling. Tonight, Lord, she needs Your peace, Your hope, and Your joy. Come and sit next to her. Wrap her in Your arms. Please help her rest tonight.*

We ask in Jesus's name, amen.

Father God, when the world feels overwhelming, help me look to You for help with . . .

who needs a break

He frequently withdrew to the wilderness to pray.

LUKE 5:16, BSB

ONCE JESUS BEGAN HIS PUBLIC MINISTRY, the crowds grew and followed Him wherever He went. He would teach, heal, and deliver hearts from pain and torment. He would rebuke, show compassion, and tell stories. He loved vibrantly and taught His disciples by example. Scripture reveals the beautiful model of Jesus's love displayed for us all to follow today.

But the Bible is also clear about another important aspect of Jesus's life and ministry: The reason He was able to continually give others His time and attention was because He leaned on the presence of the Holy Spirit and communion with His Father through prayer. We know that the Holy Spirit was with Jesus, but in addition to this constant Helper, Jesus set aside time to be alone with His heavenly Father: "He frequently withdrew to the wilderness to pray." Even after gathering a following and twelve faithful disciples, Jesus understood the value of taking a break. As mommas, this practice is imperative to our mental, emotional, and spiritual health.

One of the most poignant scenes in the Gospels is Jesus's reaction when He was told that His cousin, John the Baptist, had been killed by Herod. Upon hearing the news, Jesus attempted to find a place to be alone. But this story shows something interesting. When Jesus attempted to withdraw, the crowds followed Him. Yet He had compassion on them, taught them, and fed them. He met their needs, and only then returned to His original aim, to be alone with the Father: "After he had dismissed them, he went up on a mountainside by himself to pray" (Matthew 14:23). Jesus modeled the importance of pausing and catching our breath by taking time to be alone with our heavenly Father.

Here's what we love: Jesus didn't just model how important it was to take this time alone with God; He showed how impossible it can be. He knows what it's like when your heart is heavy and you just need a minute but those who need you are at your door. He knows what it's like to have the people you've been given to love and care for pursue you even when you need a moment of peace. We love that we have a God who knows the importance of a break but who also knows how hard it can be to find one in the middle of a busy day. We can pray from this position. We can ask God, not just to help us see the value in prayer and time alone, but to help create those moments and meet us in them.

Tomorrow, when the sun comes up, we'll be needed again. The people who call out for us or need us to feed them either physically or spiritually will be waiting for us again. God understands. He knows. And He will help us.

Tonight we pray for the momma *who needs a break. Lord, she makes so many decisions for so many people. She never stops moving. She has to stay two steps ahead of everything (even though most days she feels two steps behind). Tonight, Lord, she is tired and just needs a minute. So we ask You to do what only You can do. Make a way for this momma to have some space to breathe and meet her there. Give her peace and rest.*

We ask in Jesus's name, amen.

Lord, I need a break from . . .

_____

_____

_____

_____

_____

who is believing
for a miracle

*Jesus did many other things as well. If every one of them were
written down, I suppose that even the whole world would
not have room for the books that would be written.*

JOHN 21:25

MOMMA SAID IT WAS IMPORTANT for our clothes to be clean—
even if they weren't new—and I believed her. So my job as the oldest daughter in a family of five children was to hang clothes on the
line that stretched from our bathroom window to the neighbor's
house next door. Spring, summer, fall, and winter, I stood on the
toilet lid so I could lean out the high window to put our family's
clothes out to dry. In the winter months, the blankets, towels,
trousers, shirts, dresses, and socks would all freeze solid in the
harsh New England weather.

In the winter of 1974, my first year at college in Oklahoma,

I faced a new challenge when it came to laundering my own clothes. I didn't have much money to my name; as a matter of fact, I didn't even have enough money to wash my clothes at the dormitory laundromat. So I prayed. Have you ever believed God for something as simple as coins to do your laundry? We often believe that God works miracles only in big situations, but on my afternoon walk to class one day, I experienced His miracle-working power in the simplest of ways.

Surrounded by dozens of other students hurrying to class to get out of the cold, I was praying for the Lord to help me somehow get my clothes clean when I saw it. Lying on top of the freshly fallen snow was a crisp ten-dollar bill. There was no way to know who had dropped it or how long it had been there, but it was as though it were invisible to everyone but me. It wasn't just enough. It was more than I needed.

There are so many stories in Scripture that depict impossible situations being changed by our unstoppable God. I love reading about healings, deliverances, supernatural provision, and supernatural strength. These stories stir my faith because I remember what God said in Malachi 3:6 (NKJV): "I am the LORD, I do not change."

Did you catch that? The God who created the universe, the stars, the planets, and everything in it hasn't changed. The God who created each of us right down to our DNA and who knows every hair on our heads doesn't change. The God who healed the unhealable, changed the impossible, restored sight to the blind, and gave hope to the hopeless and life to the lifeless is the same God today.

I believe that the Lord can still intervene in any situation and change it in an instant. I believe that He can display His immeasurable power in our lives even today. And I believe that He is more than able to do all that we ask, think, or imagine and can supply every need. He is still a miracle-working God!

I have personally witnessed the physical miracles of the disabled walking, the blind eye seeing, limbs lengthened, and hearing restored. I have been the recipient of more financial miracles than I can count. I have watched as the broken and hurting have received miracles in their relationships and emotions.

John, one of Jesus's disciples, reported that "Jesus did many other things as well. If every one of them were written down, I suppose that even the whole world would not have room for the books that would be written." He is referring to the supernatural abundance of miracles that our Lord performed while on earth. Friend, Jesus is still in the miracle-working business, and we can still believe He will step into our own impossible situations.

Momma, is there something you need from Him? Is there something that only He can do? As we wrote this devotion, we paused to pray for the ones reading it. That includes you. God can meet you right now. Let's ask Him together.

Tonight we pray for the momma *who is believing for the impossible. Lord, maybe it's the miracle of peace in her heart, or maybe it's the miracle of healing for herself or someone she loves. Maybe she needs a miracle in her finances, or marriage, or she needs a way where there seems to be no way. Lord, maybe she just needs the miracle of joy in the middle of uncertainty or grief. Tonight we thank You, Lord, for being a miracle-working God. We come together in faith and ask for You to do what only You can. We believe You will.*

We ask in Jesus's name, amen.

Lord, I know that nothing is impossible for You,
so I come to You tonight asking for . . .

who needs tomorrow to be different

Brother Saul, the Lord—Jesus, who appeared to you on the road as you were coming here—has sent me so that you may see again and be filled with the Holy Spirit.

ACTS 9:17

IT WAS 2022, six months since my hysterectomy at just thirty-five, and my brain was not functioning as it had before. Every day I would wake up feeling more and more unlike myself. I struggled with short-term memory, which impacted so many areas of my life. I prayed, "Lord, how do I find my way forward?" Going back wasn't an option, but in this new normal, I needed my mental focus to be closer to how it had been before surgery. My family, my career, and my own mental health depended on it.

Do you know what happened? Day by day the Lord healed my brain and body. It was so gradual that I didn't notice at first, but when I compared how I felt nearly a year after surgery to those first few months post-operation, I saw just how far I'd come. My friend, it can be hard to be desperate for change for so long, just wishing tomorrow would be different. But perhaps today is already a little different from yesterday, and tomorrow you'll be a little closer to your miracle than where you stand right now.

A man named Saul was once in a seemingly desperate situation as well. He was a prominent religious leader who hated everything Jesus and His followers did. In fact, Saul didn't just hate them—he would seek out Christians and put them to death.

On his way to Damascus with papers granting him permission to persecute Christians in that town, Saul had an encounter with Jesus that changed his life forever.

As he neared Damascus on his journey, suddenly a light from heaven flashed around him. He fell to the ground and heard a voice say to him, "Saul, Saul, why do you persecute me?"

"Who are you, Lord?" Saul asked.

"I am Jesus, whom you are persecuting," he replied. "Now get up and go into the city, and you will be told what you must do."

ACTS 9:3-6

Saul stood up a changed man. His spiritual eyes had been opened, but he had lost his eyesight. For three days he was blind and did not eat or drink. Finally he encountered a Christian named Ananias, who greeted him this way: "Brother Saul, the Lord— Jesus, who appeared to you on the road as you were coming here— has sent me so that you may see again and be filled with the Holy Spirit."

I love that Ananias's first recorded word to Saul is "Brother." With that simple word, he accepted Saul into the fellowship of the faith. With that simple word, he acknowledged Saul's place in the body of Christ: *You are one of us now.* And then the miracle happened. "Immediately, something like scales fell from Saul's eyes, and he could see again. He got up and was baptized, and after taking some food, he regained his strength" (Acts 9:18-19).

Momma, perhaps you are like Saul tonight, waiting for your miracle. Perhaps you need a miracle when the sun comes up tomorrow. Perhaps you need someone to remind you of who you are in the body of Christ. You may need someone to say, "Sister." Maybe you need someone to tell you, "It won't always be this way. It won't always be this hard or painful. Have hope. Soon the answers will come. Everything will change. God is preparing you for what is coming next." Let's pray and believe for your miracle tonight.

Tonight we pray for the momma *who needs tomorrow to be different. Lord, she needs to wake up and find that answers have come during the night. She needs change and hope to rush in. Lord, You have a solution for what she's facing. You know how this whole situation will resolve or shift for her good. She might feel stuck, but there is joy coming in the morning, and it's going to shake things up. So tonight we ask You to meet this momma with supernatural expectancy. Fill her with hope so that as she closes her eyes, she can look forward to what will come with the morning light. Bless her.*

We ask in Jesus's name, amen.

Lord, tonight give me new eyes to see this dilemma
in my life as You see it. Show me just how far
I've come already regarding . . .

_____

_____

_____

_____

_____

_____

_____

whose heart is hurting

Jesus wept.

JOHN 11:35

"WHERE *ARE* YOU?"

If you've ever uttered that prayer, you can probably relate to the sisters Mary and Martha. Nearly a week had passed since they had sent word to Jesus that their brother, Lazarus, was sick. They were sure that if Jesus knew his dear friend was gravely ill, He would come. But He hadn't. Lazarus had passed away. He had been placed into a tomb. And four days had come and gone without the return of Jesus.

Imagine having been close to Jesus when He performed so many healing miracles. Imagine having your home be a place where He stayed during part of His ministry. Imagine knowing that if only He would hurry, He could be there in time to save your brother, whom you knew He loved. Then, after your brother died, you continued to wait for Jesus, perhaps going to the tomb to grieve as your house filled with professional mourners and your soul was exhausted from the sorrow.

But Jesus hadn't come yet. He wasn't busy, distracted, or indifferent. Far from it! Those who loved Lazarus had wanted to see a healing miracle. Jesus wanted them to witness a resurrection.

On that fourth day when the Lord arrived, the two sisters greeted Him very differently. When Jesus wasn't far from Bethany, Martha learned that He had come, and she rushed out to meet Him. She said, "Lord, if you had been here, my brother would not have died. But even now I know that whatever you ask from God, God will give you" (John 11:21-22, ESV).

There is no record of tears in Martha's plea. Instead, there was a determined resolve and confident faith that God could still do something miraculous. Jesus responded, "Your brother will rise again" (John 11:23).

Martha returned home to tell her sister, Mary, that Jesus had arrived and wanted to talk with her. Mary quickly rose and went to the place where Martha had met with Jesus. There she fell at His feet, saying, "Lord, if you had been here, my brother would not have died" (John 11:32).

Scripture records what happened then.

When Jesus saw her weeping, and the Jews who had come with her also weeping, he was deeply moved in his spirit and greatly troubled. And he said, "Where have you laid him?" They said to him, "Lord, come and see."

JOHN 11:33-34, ESV

Luke tells us that Jesus's next act wasn't raising Lazarus from the dead; instead, He paused to weep. Jesus, the One who knows all things, the One who sees the end of all things from the beginning, the One who created the world and set it into motion, stopped to cry.

He knew Lazarus would live again. He knew everything. But He stopped to weep because He was deeply moved.

Mommas, just like Mary and Martha, we sometimes don't understand the Lord's timing at all. We want Him to prevent every tragedy, sickness, and moment of pain before it happens. We wonder, "Where *were* You? Where *are* You? But just as Jesus commanded Lazarus to come forth to new life, so He can declare and speak life over every situation that is trying to overwhelm you.

Today, my friend, may I remind you that your pain still moves the heart of Jesus? He is still compassionate toward the hurt you feel. He isn't distant, removed, or cold. He hasn't turned away. He loves you and all those you love.

I hear Him reminding us that He is present even if something doesn't turn out the way we hoped. He weeps with us because our pain still moves His heart. God is "close to the brokenhearted" (Psalm 34:18). Tonight let His presence comfort you.

Tonight we pray for the momma *whose heart is hurting. Lord, remind her that the sun comes out. And she heals. And there is a day when all the pain isn't as raw, even if it's still real. Help her see where You stood and remember that even You weep, and every tear of hers You catch, and You keep. Help her know You're holding her with fire in your eyes and remind her that brokenness still breaks Your heart. This isn't some line, or some lie. Comfort her tonight as only You can and bless her as she trusts that it's all in Your hands.*

We ask in Jesus's name, amen.

Jesus, heal my heart tonight as I share it with You:

_____

_____

_____

_____

_____

who feels hopeless

When neither sun nor stars appeared for many days and the storm
continued raging, we finally gave up all hope of being saved.

ACTS 27:20

IN 2017, JARED AND I MOVED our family to California. God had
directed us there to serve at a church in the heart of Los Angeles. It
was an adventure, and it was fun, but we were there only two years
before the Lord led us to Tennessee. Two years later, the Lord led
us back home to Oklahoma.

We had sold the beautiful house we'd built when our babies were
young just before we left for California. When we returned to our
small hometown, I wished I could have it back. The truth is, I didn't
want the house back; I wanted the life I'd had before I left.

I wanted the heart full of hope and possibilities. I wanted the bank account that didn't show evidence of trusting the Lord all the way down to zero. I wanted the secure friendships and outlook that anything was possible. And despite the Lord providing us with a wonderful place to stay until we could buy our own home, I just wanted a house that was fully mine again.

I prayed for the Lord to make a way for us to have a house, but there just weren't any on the market, and we didn't have the finances on paper to be approved. Soon it had been five years since we had owned a home. It had been five years of wondering where we'd eventually settle.

It felt hopeless.

But the Lord was working out all the details. Today, only a year after returning to our small town, we have a house that is ours again. The Lord made a way behind the scenes, and despite all my feelings of hopelessness, He was setting the answer into motion.

Though my situation wasn't as dramatic as the apostle Paul's, we can see how God was also at work while Paul was a prisoner of Rome on a journey to be tried before Caesar. As Paul and his companions traveled by ship, they encountered a terrible storm: "When neither sun nor stars appeared for many days and the storm continued raging, we finally gave up all hope of being saved." The good news is that even though the ship was destroyed, no lives were lost, and a healing revival broke out on the remote island of Malta in the Mediterranean Sea where they made landfall. What seemed to be hopeless was the door to a great blessing for many, even though Paul had to endure the storm to bring it to them.

Momma, hopelessness can rise in our hearts when, like Paul, we feel surrounded by darkness as the storms of life rage on. The men on the ship with Paul did all they could to save their vessel, just as you have done everything you can think of to save your family from this trouble. But trust this: The Lord is working even now on your behalf. Hope rides even on stormy seas. He is making a way, not just for you, but for all those on the boat with you.

Tonight we pray for the momma *who feels hopeless. Lord, maybe no one knows how she feels. Maybe she hasn't even admitted it to herself. It could be her mothering or her marriage or her finances or just a little bit of everything. She's in a place that feels closed in and as if it will never resolve. But, Lord, You change everything with just a word or a moment in Your presence. Tonight we ask You to step into this momma's situation. Speak hope to her heart. Tell her what You see. And most importantly, tell her You see her. Give her peace and rest.*

We ask in Jesus's name, amen.

Jesus, hope of the hopeless,
please help me with this:

who fiercely protects those she loves

Then I, myself, will be a protective wall of fire around Jerusalem, says the LORD. And I will be the glory inside the city!

ZECHARIAH 2:5, NLT

IT WAS A SIMPLE MISUNDERSTANDING AT SCHOOL, but I (Becky) had never been in trouble before, and I was having a hard time explaining myself to the teacher through all the hot tears streaming down my face. I hadn't been to the principal's office before, and the staff had never needed to call my parents to a meeting before. It was all a big mistake, but how was I ever supposed to convince the adults in charge? I needed help. I needed an advocate. That's when my mom showed up.

My mom wore a long, red wool coat in those days. It was high fashion for Oklahoma in the midnineties and looked like something she might have worn if she had stayed in New England. I loved that coat. You couldn't miss it. It said, "I'm here," and every time my momma wore it, she meant it. She showed up fully ready to face whatever needed to be done.

I remember watching her come into the principal's office wearing that red coat and quickly getting to the bottom of the matter. I was innocent and hadn't broken any school rules, so the adults involved owed me an apology for their quick accusations.

My momma has always been a passionate protector of those she loves. I never had to face anything on my own without believing that she would come and help me if I needed her. She made that clear as I grew. She told me, "There is nothing you will face on your own that we can't figure out together."

These are the same words I say to my children today. Why? Because moms don't just protect their children from danger; we protect our children from facing the world alone. We protect our children from the pain of having to worry alone, carry their burdens alone, or work through solutions alone.

The truth is, mommas who fiercely guard their children keep a constant eye on the road in front of them, but also behind and to the sides. We pray hedges of protection around our children. We pray for God to keep them safe and surround them. We jump in when it's necessary, and sometimes before we're even asked to, not because we want to be overbearing, but because we love so deeply and care so much.

For the momma who fiercely loves her children, I must offer this important reminder: God is our protector, shield, and strength. As the Lord told His people in Jerusalem, He is "a protective wall of fire." God is the One who goes before our kids and behind our kids, keeping them in perfect peace.

If you've become weary because you have forgotten that God loves you just as fiercely as you love your children, here is a quick reminder: The armor of the Lord is your sword and your shield. Your job is to pray, trust Him, and follow His lead. His job is everything else. Let's allow God to restore our strength and bring peace to the places of our hearts that ache with worry because we've felt that protecting those we love is entirely up to us. God covers us with the red blood of His Son, and when the Lord shows up, He means it!

Tonight we pray for the momma *who fiercely protects those she loves. Lord, this momma doesn't let her children face the world alone. She is on her knees praying for them, she is keeping an eye out for potential pitfalls, and she always looks to You to be with them when she can't. Lord, this momma knows that the world is dangerous, but she serves a very big God. She knows You are the One who fights battles for her and her kids. Tonight we ask You to remind her that You are the ultimate protector and that she can trust You. She protects because she loves her kids, and You do too. Bless this momma with peace tonight.*

We ask in Jesus's name, amen.

Father, how wonderful to know that
as much as I love my children, You love them more.
Please protect them from . . .

38

who is hanging on by a thread

My Father, who has given them to me, is greater than all;
no one can snatch them out of my Father's hand.

JOHN 10:29

I WAS TEACHING MY GRANDDAUGHTER how to sew one afternoon. The day's lesson involved making some simple drapes by using the zigzag stitch on the seams. We went through the usual steps to thread the machine and began to sew. We worked a little bit and then decided we should check our work before continuing.

The top of the drape looked great with a perfect zigzag stitch, but the bottom was definitely not perfect. It was held together by only a single straight thread the length of the fabric. With a simple pull the entire thread came out. "Oh no! The bobbin is threaded incorrectly!" I exclaimed.

Even though the drapes looked perfect from the top, they were unusable. Together we spent the next ten minutes rethreading the bobbin, which involved lots of frustration and much trial and error. But finally the machine was ready to use again. When we'd finished, the zigzag on the top of the fabric matched the zigzag on the bottom of the fabric perfectly. The seam was secure.

Sometimes, as mommas, we feel like we are hanging on by only a thread. We feel as if our lives will fall completely apart with a simple pull. If one more thing goes wrong, all our hard work will be for nothing.

The truth is, the Father is holding you tightly to His heart with the power of His love. We know this because Jesus said, "My Father . . . is greater than all; no one can snatch [my followers] out of my Father's hand." When we realize that the Lord of all creation is holding on to us and we don't have to desperately hang on to a slipping thread, we will no longer worry about coming undone.

You may feel as if you cannot hold on, but His firm grasp won't let you go. No matter the difficulty of the day, week, month, or year, He's got you! You are zigzag stitched to His heart! That thread is secure.

Tonight we pray for the momma *who is hanging on by a thread. Lord, it has been a long day, and it might not have gone anything like she'd hoped. Maybe her kids are fighting or her patience is running thin. Maybe her work or marriage or money has her knotted up inside. Maybe it's all of this. Lord, tonight, no matter what is creating the threadbare places in her heart, we ask that you'd strengthen her. Fill her with a hope that surprises her. Wrap Your arms around her. You love her so much. Remind her of this now.*

We ask in Jesus's name, amen.

Jesus, please stitch me close
to Your heart and help me as I . . .

_____

_____

_____

_____

_____

_____

_____

who needs
to take a deep breath

I prophesied as he commanded me, and breath entered them;
they came to life and stood up on their feet—a vast army.

EZEKIEL 37:10

I WAS TRYING TO OUTSING KINSEY RAYMOND. That's just the
truth of it. It was 1997, and we were in the fifth-grade honor choir
together. While we had sung together in dozens of performances,
this time I decided to match her volume.

By then, I knew that Kinsey had a much louder voice than I
did. In fact, she had a much louder voice than all the children in the
choir. And every song seemed to be a self-appointed solo for Kinsey.
For some reason, that drove me crazy. It wasn't that I wanted to be
louder than her. I just didn't think it was fair that she was the only
voice that could be heard among so many. So I attempted to join her.

During this concert, if Kinsey sang loudly, I sang loudly. If Kinsey sang softly, I sang softly. I matched her throughout every song. The problem was that Kinsey sang loudly far more often than she sang softly, and I just didn't have the breath to keep up.

For years Kinsey had been taking deep breaths, forcing more air and power through her vocal cords, and training herself to carry her voice long and loud. For years she had built up the endurance required to sing that way. And as the room went dark around me and I fell face-first toward the floor, I learned just how important breath really was.

Breath is mentioned often in Scripture. One of the most notable examples involves the Old Testament prophet Ezekiel, who was once shown a vision of a valley of dry bones by the Lord, who asked him, "Son of man, can these bones live?" (Ezekiel 37:3). Then the Lord continued, "This is what the Sovereign Lord says to these bones: I will make breath enter you, and you will come to life" (Ezekiel 37:5). The Lord told Ezekiel that indeed, the bones would rise up and live again.

Momma, sometimes we feel like that valley of dry bones. Sometimes our hearts just feel weary and without life. We need to take a deep breath, but more than that, we need the breath of God to come and revive the dead places in our souls. Sometimes we just need the Lord to remind us that our weary bones can live again.

You know your own breath is important. Tonight remember that God still breathes into the wounded and weary places in your heart. You won't always feel this overwhelmed or exhausted. You won't always feel this dusty and dry. Let's ask the Father to breathe new hope and new life into the places that haven't felt fully alive in a long time. Breath matters. Friend, let's take a deep breath together.

Tonight we pray for the momma *who needs to take a deep breath. Lord, she is always thinking about something or someone. She is constantly going from one thing to the next. Sometimes she gets so busy and tense that she just forgets to breathe. Tonight we ask that You would breathe life back into her weary heart. Strengthen this momma, Lord, with Your love and Your power. Fill her with new hope. And as You come close to her right now, melt away the stress.*

We ask in Jesus's name, amen.

Holy Spirit, please breathe new life
into this part of me:

who is walking through a season of sadness

Weeping may stay for the night,
but rejoicing comes in the morning.

PSALM 30:5

As MOMMAS, we are well acquainted with tears. Whether it is bouncing an infant on our shoulders to soothe them or holding our sobbing adult children who've just suffered loss, we are the comforters of those who cry. But what happens when a momma is the one trudging through a season of sadness? What happens when she is the one shedding tears?

As an older momma, I have gone through many times of sorrow in my almost seven decades of life. I've been surrounded by that familiar mist of sadness, like a fog that doesn't seem to lift. I've felt the small warm tears of heartache landing like raindrops on my face as I've walked through difficult seasons. I've looked out at the gray haze that shadows the sunshine and washes away the peace.

For a Christian momma, seasons like these can be lonely. Being sad isn't really accepted as a hallmark of a strong Christian woman. Sadness makes others uncomfortable. They may put a time limit on our sorrow, expecting us to get it together, pull ourselves up, and be happy again. So we hide our pain. We don't want our heartache to spill over onto the feelings of others, so we try to put aside our sorrow and do our best to let others see us as victors over the mist.

But, Momma, the Bible is full of stories of people who cried. It's full of stories and poems from those who lamented. The book of Lamentations is a collection of poetry written by Jeremiah the prophet to the Lord following the fall of Jerusalem and his people's captivity in Babylon. Jeremiah cried out in Lamentations 5:15, "Joy is gone from our hearts; our dancing has turned to mourning." But the Lord heard their cries. He had a good plan for them, as He reminded His people through the weeping prophet Jeremiah's words: "'For I know the plans I have for you,' declares the LORD, 'plans to prosper you and not to harm you, plans to give you hope and a future'" (Jeremiah 29:11).

Tears are important, but they don't last forever, my friend. "Weeping may stay for the night, but rejoicing comes in the morning." You may be in a season of grief; but sorrow has an end point because joy does return. There isn't always a literal moment when the sun comes up, but joy in the truest sense comes when the Son rises and His warmth melts away the mist. In that instant, our hearts, minds, and spirits can look ahead again and see the path forward. Until then, we can trust that God is with us and will wipe away our tears.

Tonight we pray for the momma *who is walking through a season of sadness. Lord, there are so many reasons she might be sad right now. Tonight we pray this momma would know that You are with her in every moment of her journey. Melt away the mist with Your love so she can see the path forward again. Please remind her that Your joy comes in the morning and that Your plan is good.*

We ask in Jesus's name, amen.

Father, please soothe this sadness
that I'm carrying in my heart right now:

_____

_____

_____

_____

who is barely making it

This is what the LORD, the God of Israel, says:
"The jar of flour will not be used up and the jug of oil will
not run dry until the day the LORD sends rain on the land."

1 KINGS 17:14

MY HUSBAND, MARK, AND I HAVE SERVED in ministry together for many years. We've seen God do remarkable things. While the Lord has always provided for us, there were moments when our resources were slim. I remember a time when we had almost completely run out of food. All we had were a jar of pickles and a box of oatmeal.

Since it was just my husband and me, we figured we could tough it out until the next paycheck arrived. We laughed and said, "Well, if you want something salty, grab a pickle, and if you want something sweet, whip up some of the delicious oatmeal."

We told no one what was happening in our home. But that Sunday night we heard a knock at our front door. An older couple said they had been praying and decided they wanted to bless us with some groceries. They had two carloads full, including items we never bought because they were too expensive and were considered absolute luxuries. We were so blessed and knew it could only be the Lord supplying our needs.

Stories of God's provision appear throughout the Bible. It's hard to imagine anyone facing more dire circumstances than the momma in 1 Kings 17. The prophet Elijah had declared a drought upon the land because the people were worshiping false gods. The whole nation was affected, including a widow with her only son. She had used up all her resources and was desperate. On what she thought would be the day of her final meal, she went to gather sticks for the fire so she could cook one last time for herself and her son.

But the Lord had a different plan. He had instructed Elijah to go to her village, Zarephath. God told Elijah that this widow would feed him. Two completely different stories were about to come together on the outskirts of town where one momma searched for sticks.

When their paths crossed that day, Elijah asked this widow: "'Would you bring me a little water in a jar so I may have a drink?' As she was going to get it, he called, 'And bring me, please, a piece of bread'" (1 Kings 17:10-11). The widow then explained what was happening in her situation and told him about her last meal. God had a plan.

Elijah asked the momma to make him a small loaf of bread and then to make something for herself and her son. She complied with his request and brought him the loaf. Then he made an astonishing statement: "This is what the LORD, the God of Israel, says: 'The jar of flour will not be used up and the jug of oil will not run dry until the day the LORD sends rain on the land.'" In other words, the momma who was barely making it now had abundance.

Sometimes I think about how, from that day on, whenever the widow woke up and saw that again there was no rain, she knew her family's provision was secure. Isn't it interesting that God chose a season that looked dry to so many to supernaturally provide her with flour and oil?

Tonight, Momma, whatever you are facing—whether a short-term problem like trying to make it to the next paycheck on pickles and oatmeal or the devastation of a drought that has stolen all your emotional, mental, and physical resources—please remember that the God who sees all, sees your need and is able to meet it. May the oil of His provision never run out in your life.

Tonight we pray for the momma *who is barely making it. Lord, she feels like she is coming up short. Short on finances. Short on time. Short on patience. Short on hope. She needs You. She needs You to step in and make it all right. She might not even know what "all right" looks like, but You do. Because You never run short on anything. You have endless hope, strength, love, and everything she needs. Tonight You hear her cry and already have an answer for her. Meet her now.*

We ask in Jesus's name, amen.

Lord, my Provider, I ask You to supply me and my family with what we lack:

who is afraid
that she is ruining her kids

*You, Lord, are our Father. We are the clay, you are the potter;
we are all the work of your hand.*

ISAIAH 64:8

As a child of the nineties, one of my favorite gifts to receive
was a fresh pack of colorful Play-Doh. I loved opening the small,
yellow plastic cans and pulling out the perfect lump of modeling
clay. Sure, I loved that I could make anything I wanted, but what
I really loved was that the clay didn't have any flaws or marks. The
green didn't have bits of red or white left over from previous creations. Sometimes I'd wait before I made anything with the clay
because I didn't want it to be ruined. It was a clean slate, a fresh
start, and I could make it into anything I imagined.

It might seem an odd comparison, but when I brought my kids

home from the hospital, they, too, were fresh, unmarked by any-one's influence. I remember thinking that who they grew to be had so much to do with what I modeled and how I cared for them. I told myself, *I'll never yell. I'll never let them watch too much TV. I'll cook only the healthiest foods.* And then, as our life began to unfold, I realized my children weren't being raised by a saint. They were being raised by a woman who relied heavily on Jesus but still got it wrong plenty of times.

So can I speak honestly for just a moment? I wonder if you worry that your own imperfections are going to somehow prevent your children from becoming what you hope for them. I wonder if you, too, had plans for how you'd parent your kids, and you're noticing that no matter what you do, little bits of yourself are showing up in their attitudes and behaviors. You're questioning whether you're doing a good job.

Momma, God knows how hard you're trying to set good examples and good goals for your family. He knows that if love were all it took, you'd never have to worry about how anything turned out because you love your kids so much. But just as Isaiah prayed, the truth is that God is the One shaping our children alongside us.

So even when we get it wrong or make decisions we wish we could change, we can trust that the Lord knows who our children will become and knows you are the mom who can help them get there. If it were only up to us, we'd have to carry the full weight of who our children become, but they need us to be their momma . . . not their Lord. They still need Jesus to help them grow into all He has for them. You're doing a good job, friend.

Tonight we pray for the momma *who is afraid she is ruining her kids. She tries to speak softly, but sometimes she yells. She tries to cook nutritious meals, but sometimes it's just frozen pizza. She doesn't want time to pass, but sometimes she thinks, If only they were a little older. Lord, tonight we pray for this momma. Please make her path straight. Please fill her with your peace and strength. Remind her that she is trying her hardest and that You love her.*

We ask in Jesus's name, amen.

Father, please continue to mold _____
as I continue to trust You to lead me.

_____

_____

_____

_____

_____

who just needs you, Lord

Then they cried out to the Lord in their trouble,
and he delivered them from their distress.

PSALM 107:6

THE DOCTOR TOLD ME, "I think you should see a surgeon. He can tell what this lump is by doing a biopsy." I had just returned to college for my senior year, and I had not been feeling well. I called my momma to tell her that I was coming home and that I needed an appointment to see a surgeon. I said I was going to drive myself and my things home, which was just over fifteen hundred miles away, because I didn't know how long I would be out of school. She insisted that my sister fly out to help me drive, and she did. I had honestly just wanted to think about everything on my own while on the road, but in the end, I very much enjoyed my sister's company.

I met with the surgeon right away, and my fears were immediately relieved. He told me that I was fine and surgery was unnecessary. I was so grateful to know that I was okay, but I was frustrated to be missing out on my senior year.

I prayed every day while I was home that the Lord would meet me and supply every need so I could go back to school in the spring. Because I had withdrawn from the university, I needed to reapply for admission and financial aid. I asked the Lord to make a way. I needed Him to show up and fix it.

Do you know what happened? He did exactly what I asked Him to do: He made a way. I returned to school, and shortly after I arrived back in Tulsa, I met my now husband of nearly forty-five years. The Lord knew the right timing and the answers to my questions long before I did.

What do you need Him to do, Momma? What do you need Him to do in your heart tonight? Maybe you're waiting on your own diagnosis, and the surgeon hasn't called you back yet. Maybe you're waiting to see how it all turns out. You're wondering if God will deliver you from this trial. My friend, let's cling to this truth together: "They cried out to the LORD in their trouble, and he delivered them from their distress." Your deliverance is coming. God is coming just because you called.

Tonight we pray for the momma *who needs You, Lord. She needs You to show up and fix it, bring peace, or take away the fear or anxiety. She needs You to bring clarity or solve what she can't. She needs You to help her children or her marriage. She needs You to bring health or supernatural provision. She is at the end of herself and desperate for a miracle. Lord, just as she always answers when her children call to her, You always come when she calls to You. Show up now and bring everything she needs just because You love her.*

We ask in Jesus's name, amen.

Lord Jesus, tonight I need You to . . .

who is brave

"I am the Lord's servant," Mary answered.
"May your word to me be fulfilled." Then the angel left her.

LUKE 1:38

THE SUN HAD NOT COME UP on the horizon, and most folks were still asleep. It was very early dawn, but I had been awake off and on throughout the night with what I thought were false labor contractions. My husband, Mark, was scheduled to fly out at eight for a job interview in Washington, DC, that had been scheduled for months. We were hopeful that this would lead to his next career move and were excited about his prospects of landing this job.

Just before the taxi came, I put on a brave face and told Mark that I had been having more false labor pains and that after he left, I would go to the hospital to get checked out. Between you and me,

I was pretty sure Becky was on her way, but I didn't want Mark to miss this opportunity.

When his taxi pulled up, I reassured Mark one more time before he left. "I will be fine," I insisted. "I'll be home from the hospital before you land in Washington." I truly did hope he would make it back before our daughter arrived.

I'd planned to drive myself to the hospital to get checked out, but as soon as Mark's taxi pulled away, I thought, *Oh no! I'm going to need help.* I called my neighbor, who agreed to drive me to the ER.

I started to get nervous and decided to wait by our curbside mailbox while she pulled out of her garage next door. We drove the short distance to the hospital—the one with the illuminated white cross I could see in the distance from my back patio—and she dropped me off.

I was honestly terrified. I no longer felt brave. Then again, I had heard that being brave is doing what you need to do even if you are terrified. Using that definition, I surely qualified.

Everything happened quickly after that. Becky was born before noon, and Mark was home by dinnertime to meet his new daughter. His little girl stole his heart the first time he held her in my hospital room. In the end, Mark didn't get the job. The Lord had different plans for our lives.

Over the years, I have thought about another momma who was about to give birth under unusual circumstances. Mary had said her bold yes to the angel Gabriel when he foretold the birth of our Lord: "I am the Lord's servant. . . . May your word to me be fulfilled." Because of the government decree that all must register in their ancestral home to be taxed, she had traveled all the way from Nazareth to Bethlehem—the hometown of the great king David—to have her son, Jesus. The town was so crowded that she had to give birth to her child in a stable, surrounded by the animals, and then she laid Him in a manger. She was so brave.

Momma, when you need courage, the Lord will be with you. No matter what you're facing, tonight say your yes to Him.

Tonight we pray for the momma *who is brave. Lord, she may be a newborn momma, trusting You in these early days with her baby. She might be in the thick of raising active children or teenagers. Or perhaps she is an empty nester, following You into a whole new season of life. Whatever place she is in right now, she is making brave choices for her family. We place our trust in You tonight as we look ahead. Watch over us please and keep us safe.*

In Jesus's name, amen.

Lord, You promise to grant me courage
and strength as I navigate . . .

_____

_____

_____

who needs to know
that something good is coming

Do not leave Jerusalem, but wait for the gift my Father promised,
which you have heard me speak about.

ACTS 1:4

As WOMEN AND MOTHERS, we are well acquainted with seasons of waiting. Whether we carry our babies in our hearts or bodies, we wait for our children to be born. We wait through the birthing process, the adoption process, or the transition from fostering to adoption. We wait and watch as our children grow in wisdom and stature and favor with God and man (see Luke 2:52). We wait and wait some more. Sometimes, we wait with bated breath to see how God will unfold their stories . . . and our own.

The Bible is full of stories in which men and women just like us waited on God. For instance, the Israelites waited to be freed from the power of the Egyptians, and in God's perfect timing, they were set free. God's people waited to be loosed from their captivity in Babylon, and at the perfect moment, they returned to worship their God again in the Promised Land. All of creation waited for the Savior to come, and at the appointed hour, Jesus was born. Once He had come, died, and risen again, Jesus told His friends to go to Jerusalem and wait for the gift of His Spirit. And then before Jesus returned to heaven, He said He was going to prepare a place for us and instructed us to wait for His return.

Waiting for God to do what He promised can feel hard, but it can also lead to worship as we trust the Lord who always provides. Waiting can be worship when we don't fall into the trap of hopelessness but hold on to the belief that He will come through for us. Waiting can be worship when we turn our hearts toward the One who gives all good gifts and works everything out for the good of those who love Him and are called according to His purposes (see Romans 8:28).

But for our hearts to worship, we must remember this truth in our waiting: Something good is coming. Something good was coming to the nation of Israel through their freedom from the Egyptians. Something good was coming to all nations as creation waited for King Jesus to be born. Something good was coming when Jesus told His friends to wait in Jerusalem for the gift of His Spirit. Something good is still to come as we wait for Jesus's return.

We often feel the heartache and hopelessness of the in-between— the place where we are and what we hope comes next—but God sees the full plan. He knows what is coming for each of us, and we can trust that His Word is true when He declares it is a good plan. We can trust that hope is coming, peace is coming, stress is leaving. Answers will be found, joy will rise, and discouragement will go. Here is some hope to hold on to tonight, my friend: God isn't stalling; He's preparing. And what He is preparing will be very, very good. Something good is coming.

Tonight we pray for the momma *who needs to know that something good is coming. Lord, she needs hope. She needs to believe that when she wakes up tomorrow something unexpected and exciting could happen. When it all feels the same day after day, Your Word says You have a good plan for her. So tonight we pray that hope rises in her heart. We pray for her discouragement and stress to lift. We pray for peace to come. And we pray that when she goes to sleep tonight, she believes that tomorrow could be different in the best possible way.*

We ask in Jesus's name, amen.

Jesus, please fill my heart with anticipation
and help me to trust that You have good planned
for me even as I wait for . . .

who is worn weary

*Simon answered and said to Him, "Master, we have toiled all night
and caught nothing; nevertheless at Your word I will let down the net."*

LUKE 5:5, NKJV

IF I CLOSE MY EYES, I can still hear the seagulls and feel the breeze
coming in off the bay that led to the ocean in the small New
England town where I grew up. I can remember walking across the
docks and looking down between the planks at the dark, cold water
and the green seaweed swirling around the piers.

Fishing in my community was not just a pastime but a way
many fathers made a living and fed their families. There were
so many fishermen in my town that when I read Luke 5:5, I can
almost hear Simon Peter's voice answering Jesus, "Master, we've
worked hard all night and haven't caught anything."

Simon was a fisherman by trade. He knew the long hours that began before the sun rose and sometimes carried on long into the night. He knew the rhythm of casting and hauling in nets. He knew the water. He knew the fish. So when Jesus told him to "launch out into the deep and let down [his] nets for a catch" (Luke 5:4, NKJV), he knew it was hopeless.

Simon had fished all night. He had already put in so much work. But he didn't tell Jesus no. He replied, "Master, we have toiled all night and caught nothing; nevertheless at Your word I will let down the net." He did what Jesus directed, and then came the supernatural blessing of an overflowing catch of fish. It was this miracle that caused Simon Peter to follow Jesus and change his entire life.

Momma, perhaps you are tired like Simon was. Perhaps you have toiled through many hard nights and have not seen the blessing or the promise of provision or peace or whatever you are working so hard for in life. You know the rhythm of your days. You know what it looks like to cast your net and try and try again.

Let me say to you tonight: Just as Jesus knew where the fish could be found, He knows where your strength will come from. He can provide supernatural abundance for you. Maybe you're like the hardworking fishermen in my town or Peter in this story. Maybe you have reached the end of your own strength. Maybe you're completely and utterly exhausted. That's okay. The Lord is calling you to trust Him. He wants you to believe that He is still speaking to your heart, showing you how to navigate the waters of your life.

It may feel hopeless, but may the response of your heart tonight be, "Nevertheless at Your word I will let down the net."

Nevertheless I will keep loving these kids.
Nevertheless I will trust You.
Nevertheless I will put my hope in You.
Nevertheless I will rely on You for my strength.

Just wait and see, Momma. God knows you've tried so hard and given it all you have. Now let Him surprise you with an abundance of just what you need.

Tonight we pray for the momma *who is worn weary. Lord, there aren't enough words to describe just how spread thin she feels. She is so grateful for the life she has and the family You've given her, but if she could just get a moment to breathe, she'd really appreciate it. Lord, tonight we ask for You to do something supernatural. In the middle of her exhausting and busy schedule, meet her with rest. Fill her with strength, peace, and hope for the days ahead. Help her sleep soundly tonight.*

We ask in Jesus's name, amen.

Jesus, my heart may be heavy
and my mind restless; nevertheless . . .

who has a fiery daughter

Villagers in Israel would not fight; they held back until I,
Deborah, arose, until I arose, a mother in Israel.

JUDGES 5:7

I HAVE RAISED A FIERY DAUGHTER. Have you? Once at the grocery store, when my daughter was still young enough to ride in the cart alongside her little brother, an older woman commented on how sweet my son was. This woman, known in our community for her kindness, said to him, "I'll just take you home with me."

My quick-minded and fierce little girl who didn't understand this woman's intentions answered, "No you won't. He's my brother." And she meant it. She is a fighter for justice and keeper of the score always. She knows her own mind, and she knows what's right.

Scripture doesn't tell us much about what Deborah was like as a little girl. We don't know if she was timid or bold. We don't know if she was outspoken or reserved. We don't know if she followed the rules or rebelled. But we do know that she grew up to become a woman honored by her community and given authority to rule.

In Scripture, Deborah is one of the only women called a prophet, which means that she heard from God and shared His words with the people. She is also called a judge: "Now Deborah, a prophet, the wife of Lappidoth, was leading Israel at that time. She held court under the Palm of Deborah between Ramah and Bethel in the hill country of Ephraim, and the Israelites went up to her to have their disputes decided" (Judges 4:4-5). Deborah's voice was greatly respected, finding favor not just among the common people in her kingdom but also among those in leadership.

One time Barak, a ruler of Israel, said he would not even go to war unless Deborah went with them. When she said, "Go!" the people went. When she gave judgment, they listened. When she shared the heart of God, they obeyed. She was a woman full of fire and justice, and the Lord was with her.

I think of Deborah's mom as I raise my own fiery daughter. She didn't put out the fire that burned in her daughter's heart or snuff out the flame of justice and honor. Deborah sat in a place of judgment because she had not been confined to a place of complacency. Armies won battles because of her wisdom, and there was peace in the land for forty years because of her leadership.

We need Deborahs today. We need women unafraid of stepping into the places of authority God has given them; women willing to use bold, wise words to speak about the things He places on their hearts. And as mommas raising the next generation of women leaders, we need to protect the passion ablaze in our girls. We need to make sure they, too, can fulfill what God has called them to because we haven't "corrected" them into complacency.

I know what it's like to raise a girl who questions if what she has been told is good and true. I know what it is like to raise a daughter who fights for what is best. I know what it is like to raise a daughter who is strong. I also know that God has placed within you and me the exact characteristics to parent fiery daughters. He knew we'd need patience and perseverance. He knew we'd need strength and tenderness. He knew they'd need mommas like us. He knew He could trust us to protect the flame of faith.

Tonight we pray for the momma *raising one or more fiery daughters. Lord, You know how carefully these girls must be led. You created them with fierce passion that shouldn't be put out or contained. So often their determination doesn't come from a strong will or a disobedient heart but from a passion put there by You, God. You created strong girls to ignite movements, to kindle hope, and to warm the lonely. Lord, help this momma lead her daughter well. Give her wisdom, patience, tenderness, and compassion. The world needs girls with fire in their hearts now more than ever. You knew this momma was the one for the job. Give her rest tonight.*

We ask in Jesus's name, amen.

Jesus, please help me to raise _____
with wisdom, patience, tenderness, and compassion.

who has a determined son

*When Elizabeth heard Mary's greeting, the baby leaped in her womb,
and Elizabeth was filled with the Holy Spirit.*

LUKE 1:41

THERE IS A SAYING that boys will turn your hair gray. If Elizabeth, the mother of John the Baptist, had not already been an old, white-haired woman before she became pregnant, her son likely would have given her plenty of grays. Before John was born, an angel had appeared to Elizabeth's husband, Zechariah, and said, "He [John] will be a joy and delight to you, and many will rejoice because of his birth, for he will be great in the sight of the Lord. . . . He will be filled with the Holy Spirit even before he is born. He will bring back many of the people of Israel to the Lord their God" (Luke 1:14-16).

John surely was a joy to his parents, but his life was far from ordinary. He let his momma know when he was still in her womb that he was full of destiny and God's purpose. When Mary, the mother of Jesus, visited Elizabeth while they were both pregnant, she greeted Elizabeth, causing John, already full of the Holy Spirit, to leap in his mother's womb.

When John grew up, he was so determined to announce the coming of our Lord that he preached in the wilderness and survived on locusts and wild honey. He wore camel's hair clothing and a leather belt. He preached repentance to all who sought him out, and he baptized many. He wasn't afraid to call out sin wherever he saw it, including in the religious and political leaders. John's life provides a clear picture of being a determined son.

Momma, raising a determined son is a high calling. It is not an easy task and can be quite challenging. But remember that the Lord picked you to be your son's momma, just like he chose Elizabeth to be John the Baptist's momma. He knows exactly who you are and exactly who your son is. He knows who your son will grow up to be. You can trust in the Lord as you watch Him fulfill your child's destiny.

Tonight we pray for the momma *of a determined son. Lord, there is nothing quite like the relationship between a momma and her little boy, no matter his age. From the time he was born, this mom knew her heart would never be the same. Her son is fearless, adventurous, and brave. And each day she prays that You would help her know exactly how to help him become the man You created him to be. This momma needs strength, peace, and sometimes a strong cup of coffee to keep her on her toes, but she wouldn't trade a moment of it. Bless this momma and her son(s).*

We ask in Jesus's name, amen.

Father, please direct and protect this determined boy in my life:

who needs to know you're close

The LORD is near to all who call on him,
to all who call on him in truth.

PSALM 145:18

"Mooooommmmmaaaaa!!!"

His voice seemed far away as I sat up and tried to clear my head. I climbed out of bed, felt my way across my room in the dark, and headed toward his bedroom. "I'm coming!" I shouted as I navigated through the living room and kitchen. "What is it? Are you okay?" I asked before I even got to my eight-year-old.

"I need water."

I put my wrist across his forehead. He needed more than water. He was burning up. I gave him a drink and some fever reducer, adjusted his blankets, and sat at the end of his bed until he fell back asleep. But even then, I didn't go back to bed. I kept watch over him throughout the night. I stayed close.

I've run through the house in the middle of the night for all three of my children. I've run when they call out because they're having a bad dream. I've run when they are sick and need someone to help them. I've run just because they're awake and alone and the world feels strange when all the lights are off. I've run to the school to pick them up when they're ill. I've run to their friends' houses when they just want to come home. When our children call for us, we go because we are momma and that's what momma does.

My friend, do you love your children more than God loves you? It's not a trick question. Consider it as if you do not know the answer for just a moment. In your humanity, could you ever love your children more than the eternal, perfect God loves you? Our overflowing love for our kids cannot compare to the love of God for us. As much as you love your children, God's love for you is greater still!

He is a good Father. His love for you is forever. You don't have to call just right, think just right, act just right, pray just right, or be just right for Him to decide that you're worth His presence. Jesus died on the cross just so He could be with you. That was the purpose of His life, death, and resurrection. God's Son came down from heaven so He could remain close to me and you forever: "For God so loved the world that he gave his one and only Son, that whoever believes in him shall not perish but have eternal life" (John 3:16). That eternal life is with Him—not just in the place where He lives but in His forever presence.

You have access to the presence of God right now. You have access to His love right now. "The LORD is near to all who call on him, to all who call on him in truth."

He is close to you in this moment. He is close to you through every joy, sadness, and suffering. His presence walks you through it all. You can call on Him, and remember: He knows exactly what you need in this moment.

Tonight we pray for the momma *who needs to know that You are close. Lord, she needs to know that You are right here with her in the middle of every heartache, sadness, challenge, and discouragement. Lord, we ask that she would feel Your presence with her right now and know that she is not alone. We ask for sweet, restorative rest. We thank you in advance for every answer, and we believe for every promise.*

We pray in Jesus's name, amen.

Abba, Father, make Your presence known
to me now as I call out to You about . . .

_____

_____

_____

_____

who needs your peace

Do not let your hearts be troubled.
You believe in God; believe also in me.

JOHN 14:1

IT WAS 1974 and I was getting on an airplane for the very first time. I wasn't going on a short trip or quick vacation to a neighboring state. I was traveling from Bristol, Rhode Island, to Tulsa, Oklahoma—a city and state I had never even visited—to start my freshman year of college. Truthfully, I wasn't even sure where the university was in relation to the airport. But I had two suitcases, my ticket, and fifty dollars in the bank; and I was following the Lord's direction.

A relative had driven me and my parents to Boston Logan Airport. In those days, anyone could walk up to the gate. I watched my parents standing at the plate glass window as the plane pulled away. They were waving, and I was pretty sure my mom was crying. But I was off on a great adventure that would change the course of my whole life. And I had peace.

When I think about it even to this day, I don't know how I did it. How had I gotten on that plane? How had I decided to leave everything familiar and travel over fifteen hundred miles to a place unknown? After all, I had suffered from anxiety since childhood. But the peace of God just came over me, and I got on the plane, found my seat, and landed in Tulsa a few hours later for the start of an amazing life journey.

You know, sometimes we experience a peace that baffles the understanding. It doesn't make sense to anyone else. Have you ever experienced this? Maybe someone you love was in the hospital or received a difficult diagnosis, yet you trusted God's care. Maybe you were moving across country, but trusted that God was leading you. Maybe you were switching careers, but despite the unknown, you felt calm about the change.

Sometimes peace comes and confounds the wisdom of man. In other seasons, peace seems so elusive, and you are up at night praying and crying out to God for answers and help. Whichever situation you are in tonight, we ask that you invite Jesus, the Prince of Peace, to come and blanket your heart and home with His comfort and rest.

Momma, tonight we pray for you, that in times of great turmoil or great decisions, the peace of our Lord would wash over your heart and mind. Just as Jesus spoke over His disciples, we believe He is speaking to you. He says, "Do not let your hearts be troubled. You believe in God; believe also in me." Whatever is troubling you, we pray that your heart would be still and filled with the peace that only He can bring.

Tonight we pray for the momma *who needs Your peace. Lord, so much in her life feels unsettled, and the world seems like such a turbulent place right now. So many things are outside her control. She asks for peace in her own heart and mind. She asks for Your peace to blanket her heart and home. Lord, we ask that You meet her right where she is, wherever that may be, and fill her heart with the peace that passes all understanding.*

We ask in Jesus's name, amen.

Lord, please fill me with Your peace about . . .

who feels stretched thin

While Jesus was in Bethany in the home of Simon the Leper,
a woman came to him with an alabaster jar of very expensive perfume,
which she poured on his head as he was reclining at the table.

MATTHEW 26:6-7

MY MOM AND I BOTH LOVE the movie *The Fellowship of the Ring.*
You've probably seen or at least heard of it. It's part of The Lord of
the Rings series. In the film, a group of friends set out on a mission
to stop evil, but it requires their combined efforts and strength. At
the beginning of the journey, as the burden of the mission passes
from one generation to the next, a kind old man sits down in a chair
and tells his friend, "I feel thin, sort of stretched like butter scraped
over too much bread. I need a holiday. A very long holiday."*

---

* The Fellowship of the Ring, directed by Peter Jackson (Burbank, CA: New Line Cinema, a unit of Warner Bros. Pictures Group, 2001).

I was much younger when I first saw this movie, but as I have aged, those words resonate deeply in my own heart. I, too, feel stretched thin. I feel like there's not enough of me to cover all that needs to be done.

Every day mommas wake up and start over. Sometimes the night slips right into the morning with no break in between. We use our strength and love to take care of all our family's needs. We don't keep anything in reserve. We pour out our care and concern for our family in a myriad of ways.

The Bible records the story of a woman who showed her love for Jesus by pouring out a precious jar of expensive perfume on His head as He reclined at a dinner table. Not everyone was moved by her extravagant gesture. "When the disciples saw this, they were indignant. 'Why this waste?' they asked" (Matthew 26:8). The disciples should have known better, but they complained that the perfume could have been sold and the money given to the poor. Only Jesus knew that what this woman had done was more than an act of sacrifice—it was part of the preparation for His coming crucifixion: "Why are you bothering this woman? She has done a beautiful thing to me. The poor you will always have with you, but you will not always have me" (Matthew 26:10-11).

Momma, not everyone will understand that you are happy to give your best to your children. They may think that you could pour out your life someplace better while bringing in more financial resources for your family. But the Lord values the extravagant love that others may consider a waste of your time and talents. In fact, He can supernaturally increase what you offer to those you love.

You and I may feel stretched thin, but when we remember the arms of Jesus stretched on Calvary's cross, we remember that extravagant love always comes at an extravagant price. When you feel spread thin, the Lord will make up the difference by giving you His strength and filling you with His love.

Tonight we pray for the momma *who feels stretched thin. Lord, every day presents a new set of challenges, and she does her best to face each one as it comes. But sometimes she feels like a blanket that can't quite cover everyone who needs her. Lord, she needs Your help tonight. Remind her that You shield her and her family. Strengthen her and fill her with hope.*

We ask in Jesus's name, amen.

Lord Jesus, please provide in these places
where I feel spread thin:

_____

_____

_____

_____

_____

who wishes she could see to the other side

*All the days ordained for me were written
in your book before one of them came to be.*

PSALM 139:16

"ARE YOU READY?" I called out to my husband.

"Yep," he said. "Let's go, Susan."

A few days earlier, Mark had gone to see a dermatologist who'd performed a skin biopsy. For weeks prior to that appointment, I had been asking him to see a doctor about the large growth on his face. When we left the house that morning to hear the results of the biopsy, I was just ready to have this in the past and move on. We thought at worst the growth might be a basal cell carcinoma, which is often easily treatable.

The doctor's office was gray. That's what I remember most

thirty years later. We walked into the exam room, and I sat in the extra chair—you know, the one for family members who are just there for support. The doctor came into the room, greeted us, and then took a marker and drew a line from my husband's ear to his jaw and then up the other side.

The doctor explained that what we'd thought might be a basal cell carcinoma was actually eccrine (sweat gland) carcinoma. It was a much larger and more concerning diagnosis that would require an intensive treatment.

In that moment, the room got really dark, and the world just sort of stopped. I had a thousand questions, but my first task was to breathe. That day, we began a journey that I had not prepared myself to take. All I wanted to do was see the other side of this challenge and know what the outcome would be.

Maybe you know what that feels like. My friend, I wish I could tell you that my faith rose up like a lion and I declared healing and wholeness, praying powerfully for my husband. But honestly, we had two little girls and I was scared.

During that time, a friend reminded me that someday I would look back on this and see the Lord's hand on the situation. She was right. My husband successfully completed treatment and has had no recurrence of the disease. Over the years, I have held on to my friend's words, thinking about them countless times. That's especially true when I look at my husband and ask him, "Are you ready?" as we head out the door.

Friend, whatever you are going through, whatever stands square in front of you that seems to block your view, let me be the one to say that God knows all your days, and He sees when this trial will end. It may feel as if it will never resolve, but there will be a time when it is over. As the psalmist says, "All the days ordained for me were written in your book before one of them came to be." We can trust Him with each one. Even when we can't see to the other side, we can keep our eyes locked on Him. Let's lean into that truth tonight as we pray together.

Tonight we pray for the momma *who wishes she could see to the other side. Lord, she wants so badly to know what's up ahead. She wants to know how it works out, how You come through, and how Your promises will be fulfilled in her life. Lord, she keeps peering into the future, but it all seems fuzzy. Tonight we ask that You help her find the strength to let go of what might be. Help her find peace with You in this moment, even if she can't see what's next. You know what's coming, and in that she can rest.*

In Jesus's name we pray, amen.

Father, help me to trust that You
are working in and through this struggle in my life:

who is lonely

"How do you know me?" Nathanael asked.
Jesus answered, "I saw you while you were still
under the fig tree before Philip called you."

JOHN 1:48

I HAVE A PHOTOGRAPH OF ME looking out the window of our second-floor apartment at the snow on the ground. When I look at it, the picture takes me back to that season over thirty years ago. Our older daughter was just a few months old, and we had moved to this city less than a year before. My family was far away, and my husband's family was very busy. We had not settled into a church home, nor had I found my stride as a brand-new momma. I can hardly bear to look at my face in that photo because I remember the profound loneliness I felt in that apartment. In that season, I felt hidden away and unseen.

After years of praying for young moms, I now know that what I was experiencing was fairly common. My circumstances were unique to me, but intense loneliness is something that so many mothers experience.

Have you experienced your own season of loneliness? It could be that your newborn is premature or sick, or that you don't have transportation to get to gatherings. Maybe you lack the finances or haven't yet found your tribe of friends. Perhaps your church home doesn't have a ministry for your stage of life. Maybe your children have left home or are away at events most evenings. Motherhood is full of seasons of loneliness.

When I feel isolated or alone, it helps me to remember the story of Nathanael, who would become one of Jesus's disciples. One day his friend Philip showed up and encouraged him to come and meet Jesus. "When Jesus saw Nathanael approaching, he said of him, 'Here truly is an Israelite in whom there is no deceit'" (John 1:47). When Nathanael asked Jesus how He knew him, "Jesus answered, 'I saw you while you were still under the fig tree before Philip called you.'" Though John doesn't tell us what Nathanael was doing under that tree, many scholars believe that he regularly went to this private place to pray.

Why is the interaction between Jesus and Nathanael important? Because just like Nathanael, the Lord sees you! He saw Nathanael when he was doing what he likely did every day—praying. The Lord sees you when you do the very things you do every day. He sees you in the most ordinary moments, even the ones that are overlooked by everyone else. Whether loneliness defines this season or is something you've been through in the past, the Lord has helpers and answers for you. Let's pray tonight for the Lord to continue to bring healing to every area of life in which we feel alone.

Tonight we pray for the momma *who is lonely. Lord, she is often surrounded by people, whether her children, coworkers, or family, but her heart often feels isolated. She feels unseen, unheard, and unimportant. Lord, she wishes others really saw the hurting places in her heart so she wouldn't have to carry this alone. She needs to know You see each lonely moment, secret pain, and unseen scar. She needs Your peace and the comfort of Your Presence. Please help her know tonight that she's never really alone. You are with her even now.*

We ask in Jesus's name, amen.

Jesus, I ask You to fill these places in me and my life that feel unseen, ignored, or underappreciated:

_____

_____

_____

_____

who tries her hardest

*David said to Saul, "Your servant used to keep sheep for his father.
And when there came a lion, or a bear, and took a lamb from the flock,
I went after him and struck him and delivered it out of his mouth."*

1 SAMUEL 17:34-35, ESV

SEVERAL YEARS AGO, a video circulated online of a man walking
away from a mountain lion down a trail back toward his vehicle.
He yelled, threw stones, and made himself bigger. He never
turned away from the lion but steadily filmed the entire event as
he retreated to safety. We know he made it because we've seen the
recorded proof. We've seen several videos like this. The ones who
survived encounters with wild animals were those who remained
calm until they were able to escape.

King David was a man of steady heart and mind. Long before
he took the throne and ruled Israel, he tended sheep for his family.

Sometimes a lamb was attacked by a lion or a bear. According to 1 Samuel 17, David did not play dead, nor did he run. He remained calm.

He explained, "I went out after him, and smote him, and delivered it out of his mouth: and when he arose against me, I caught him by his beard, and smote him, and slew him" (1 Samuel 17:35, KJV). I like that word *smote*; it's so much more elegant than *punched*. But let's remember something: We are talking about wild animals. David didn't run but confronted these threats to his sheep. He clubbed the bear and grabbed the lion by its beard, which was very close to its massive teeth. But according to Scripture, the lion dropped the lamb and David proceeded to kill the beast.

Now what does all this lion and bear (oh my!) talk have to do with us as mommas? When I think of a momma who tries her hardest, I think of King David. I think of women who face whatever comes with all the strength we have. We know that the Lord is with us, and though we might be afraid, we handle whatever needs to be done.

That's you, my friend. You manage the situation with the Lord's help. It could be a difficult job that you keep working at to put food on the table, or it could be the exhaustion you feel when your baby finally drifts off to sleep or when you've finished helping with the homework and your teenagers have turned out their lights. It could be sickness or discouragement; but you keep going and you chase that bear or lion with prayer and your reliance on the Lord. For the momma who tries her hardest, remember that you aren't shepherding your flock on your own. The Lord is with you. He will give you strength.

Tonight we pray for the momma *who tries her hardest every day. Lord, she gives and pours and does all the things, and most of the time she wonders if it's ever enough. She questions whether or not her family knows just how much she thinks, worries, and prays for them every single day. Tonight, Lord, we ask You to lean in and speak peace to her heart. You see everything she does, and You celebrate her. You are proud of her. Help her feel Your love tonight.*

We ask in Jesus's name, amen.

Lord, help me to trust that You can tame
these "lions" and "bears" in my life:

_____

_____

_____

_____

_____

who is holding her breath

Let everything that has breath praise the LORD.

Praise the LORD.

PSALM 150:6

AS A KID IN THE MIDSIXTIES, I often went to a beach called Green Grass in my hometown. I know, that's an odd name for a beach, but on this coast of Rhode Island, there was a long stretch of green grass, two feet of sand, and then—*boom*—the bay. Back then, adults were busy being adults while the kids were busy being kids, which meant that we had to look out for one another. This is important because although I enjoyed going to Green Grass, I did not know how to swim, and this beach didn't have any lifeguards. What Green Grass did have was a giant boulder jutting out about fifteen yards into the water. And all the kids loved jumping off it and swimming back to the sandy shore.

Since I didn't know how to swim, I didn't go out that far. I mostly stayed close to the beach and had fun. But one afternoon a few kids decided to help me out to the rock. They each took an arm, and off we went. The trouble was that once we reached the boulder, they forgot I couldn't swim and paddled away.

As I stood there wondering what to do, a line of children formed behind me. They were waiting their turn to jump in. Kids were diving off in every direction. I didn't move, but the next thing I knew, I was in the water. Actually, I was under the water and splashing furiously trying to surface.

I popped up once, then twice, gasping for air, and then suddenly I was being pulled to shore. An older girl wearing a pink swim cap dragged me to the beach. I must have swallowed a pint of water, but once safely on the sand I finally caught my breath.

Have you ever found yourself underwater, unable to breathe? Or maybe, friend, you weren't anywhere near water, but you were holding your breath through a hard season of life. Sometimes that's all you can do. The moments I was under the dark waters at Green Grass were not the time to breathe, but once I made it safely to shore, it was time to take a breath again.

Here is something important to know: When you've been holding your breath for answers that finally come, it's okay to inhale and exhale again; when you get through that hard moment or shift in seasons, it's okay to breathe again. It would have been pretty silly of me to sit on that sand and refuse to breathe. No, I was gasping for air and choking out the salty water I'd swallowed.

Tonight you don't have to continue holding your breath. We pray that the Holy Spirit would fill your lungs to fullness and give you new strength and power. We pray that you would not remain breathless but would be rescued from whatever is trying to sink you in this season, whatever is weighing on your heart. Then you can join the psalmist who said, "Let everything that has breath praise the LORD. Praise the LORD."

Tonight we pray for the momma *who is holding her breath, waiting to see how it all turns out. Lord, this momma needs help, hope, or a miracle. She needs You to step in, to reach into her situation and rescue her, or to simply resolve what's weighing on her heart. Tonight, Lord, please remind her that she doesn't have to remain breathless, that Your Holy Spirit can fill her with Your power and strength, and that she can be strong in You. Bless her tonight.*

We pray in Jesus's name, amen.

Holy Spirit, help me to inhale Your grace and peace
as I release these worries to You:

_____

_____

_____

who is tired of uncertainty

*She was so overjoyed she ran back without opening it
and exclaimed, "Peter is at the door!"*

ACTS 12:14

"GOOD AFTERNOON. This is Crystal Bellmore calling." The voice
mails all began the same way. Crystal was the information liaison
for the district where my kids attended school in March 2020, and
each of her automated and prerecorded phone calls brought a new
level of uncertainty to our already disrupted lives.

Her first call informed us that a parent in the district had tested
positive for the COVID-19 virus and had been in a school building
while symptomatic. Due to privacy concerns, Crystal couldn't tell us
which building the parent had visited, but she let us know that every
school in the district would be closed until they could all be cleaned.

As the events of that month unfolded across the world, Crystal called to let us know that the schools would stay closed "for just a few more weeks." As the reopening date approached, we received another automated call informing us that state government was recommending all schools stay closed until further notice.

As parents, we just wanted our children to be safe. That time was full of unanswered questions and chaos. We didn't know what was coming next, but we wanted to make the right choices for our kids. All we could do was trust God and pray.

The early church also faced a time of great unpredictability shortly after James, the brother of John, had been captured and put to death by the sword. Now the authorities had placed Peter in chains and put him in prison under guard. There was much persecution of the church by the religious and government leaders. Everyone was waiting to see what would happen next.

The authorities planned to put Peter on trial after the Feast of the Passover. Meanwhile, "the church was earnestly praying to God for him" (Acts 12:5). To those on the outside, the power seemed to be with those keeping Peter bound, but the church knew who the source of their true strength was. So they prayed.

While they were praying, the answer was already on its way. An angel had come to the prison and brought Peter past the gates and guards and through the city to safety. When he arrived at the house where the people were praying, Peter knocked. Rhoda, a servant, came to the door. "When she recognized Peter's voice, she was so overjoyed she ran back without opening it and exclaimed, 'Peter is at the door!'"

Momma, in the times of greatest trouble, the most powerful weapon we have is the power of prayer. The apostle Paul reminds us: "The weapons we fight with are not the weapons of the world. On the contrary, they have divine power to demolish strongholds" (2 Corinthians 10:4). Just like the early church prayed for Peter and the angel came to release him from prison, our prayers have the power to pull down anything that has a stronghold in our lives.

Tonight we encourage you to wield the most powerful weapon of prayer against difficulty and confusion. Watch as the answers come. Recognize them. Open the door and receive them.

Tonight we pray for the momma *who is tired of uncertainty. Lord, life lately has been a lot. It has been full of unanswered questions, second-guessing, and unexpected change. She's tired of wondering and waiting. There is a lot taking place in her heart and home, and she needs the assurance that You have it all under control. Lord, please be with this momma tonight. Please be her hope and peace. Help her rest and know that You are working it out.*

We ask in Jesus's name, amen.

Father, thank You for remaining constant despite
the world changing around me. Help me see that
You have these issues under control:

who feels like she doesn't have much to offer

In the beginning God created the heavens and the earth.

GENESIS 1:1

WHEN MY OLDER DAUGHTER WAS BORN, I wanted her nursery to be perfect. That included buying matching sheets, curtains, bath towels, and little facecloths. There was an attractive changing table with a place for the baby powder and all the extras that newborns and infants need. The rocking chair, which was a gift from a friend, was my absolute favorite item in the room, and my daughter and I spent hours rocking in that chair together. I was making a home for her by creating a special place. The thought and care I put into it were intentional because I loved her so much.

God did the same for us. The Bible opens by telling us that "in the beginning God created the heavens and the earth." Do you see what He did? He created a space for us to live. He filled it with everything we would need, and He placed the first man, Adam, and the first woman, Eve, in the Garden of Eden. He met with them there in the cool of the day.

Every letter in the Hebrew language developed from a pictograph—a picture that depicts an object or an idea. The first word in the Bible begins with the Hebrew letter *bet*. It's a picture of a house or home. Amazing! From the beginning of creation, from the first letter of His Word, God created for us a home, the earth, and settled us into this heavenly universe. He created a place for our stories to be told, especially the story of salvation.

Momma, your love is like that. You love your children so much that the first thing you did was create a space for them in your home, a place where they would be safe and know that they are loved. When we make a space for those we love, we are truly reflecting our Creator's care for us. You may wonder whether you did enough today, but the big picture shouts that you do so much more than enough for your family. They are loved, they are safe, and they are home.

Tonight we pray for the momma *who feels like she doesn't have much to offer. Lord, she does her best to create a space for her family to feel loved and safe. She tries to give them everything she can. She pours her heart out in every way possible but sometimes wonders if her love is enough. Tonight we ask You to remind her that Your love for her and her children is more than enough. You help her lead them, provide for them, and give them a home. Help this momma to rest tonight. Give her strength and peace for tomorrow.*

We ask in Jesus's name, amen.

Lord, I want to create a home that reflects
Your love and care. Please help our home be
a place our family can . . .

who is a nana

*I am reminded of your sincere faith, which first lived
in your grandmother Lois and in your mother Eunice
and, I am persuaded, now lives in you also.*

2 TIMOTHY 1:5

WHEN I PLAYED WITH my grandson Jaxton yesterday, I remembered a long-ago day I spent with my own nana. We sat on a bench under the shade of a pear tree. The birds were singing, and the breeze from the bay made the leaves cast dancing shadows on the ground. The sky was filled with those cotton candy clouds that remind you of balloons and pirate ships. My nana took the time to just sit with me. In these quiet moments I knew that I was important and loved. This is one of my favorite childhood memories. It is simple yet profound.

As Jaxton and I shot Nerf darts down the hallways and then

colored at my kitchen table, I realized that this might be an after-noon he remembers when he looks back on the story of his life—a simple time of just being with his nana.

Perhaps you have a special memory of your grandmother that makes you smile. Maybe she was your person to talk to when you had no one else, or she cooked or sewed or showed up to all your games and performances. Nanas bring joy to our families in so many ways.

One particular grandmother in Scripture teaches us the impor-tance of generational faith. On his second missionary journey, the apostle Paul had a traveling companion named Timothy who later went on to become the leader of the church at Ephesus. When Paul wrote a letter of encouragement to him, he was careful to mention Timothy's grandmother, Lois. He said, "I am reminded of your sincere faith, which first lived in your grandmother Lois and in your mother Eunice and, I am persuaded, now lives in you also." Paul gave Lois such high praise when he described her faith and its effect on Timothy.

I've heard it said that there are no second-generation Christians. By this we mean that each person must experience rebirth in Christ for themselves. Yet we can still pass on a legacy of faith, trusting that our own sons and daughters will come to know the Lord after us. What a heritage to have lived with faith so great that our grand-children and great-grandchildren will come to know the Lord because He was first seen in us!

You might not have grandchildren yet, or perhaps your home is full of them. But in either case, the children in your home are watching, learning, and feeling their heavenly Father's love through your own. Tonight let's pause and offer a prayer of thanks for the women who have been grandmothers of the faith before us.

Tonight we pray for every nana *in our lives. She may be called* _____. *Her love and devotion, care and concern, words of wisdom and helping hands make our families stronger. Lord, we ask that You bless each of these women tonight. Please fill their hearts with joy. Help them know how much we love them.*

We ask in Jesus's name, amen.

Thank you, Lord, for _____, who impacted my life by . . .

_____

_____

_____

_____

who has nothing left to give

Come with me by yourselves to a quiet place and get some rest.

MARK 6:31

IT WAS A WARM SUMMER EVENING when the sky stays lit well past bedtime for two small preschoolers. I opened the garage door and dragged two Power Wheels motorized cars (gifts from grandparents) from behind the mess of lawn equipment and paint buckets.

This was Kolton and Kadence's favorite time of day. They loved making the loop around our neighborhood block as I chased behind them shouting directions: "Slow down!" "Don't crash into each other!" "Don't hit the neighbor's parked car!" Our quiet street was disturbed with the happiest chaos in those evening hours.

When I look back, summer nights like these hold some of my favorite memories from that season of life. But as I lived them? I felt the full exhaustion of caring for three small children under six. It was a time in which I daily offered my little bits of strength, hope, and joy to the Lord, trusting that He would meet me and supernaturally multiply all I offered Him.

Are you in a season of loving your children but feeling wholly exhausted? Motherhood in every season is holy work and often hard work. God invited us into this calling of caring for our kids, and everything He calls us to requires us to lean fully on Him. The disciples knew this was true.

When Jesus sent His disciples to tell others the Good News, they were faithful in their mission. They did just as He commanded. They had drawn large crowds, and they were tired—so tired, in fact, that Scripture says they hadn't even had a chance to eat.

Seeing this, the Lord invited them to go with Him to a quiet place where they could get some rest. Pardon me while I pause the story right here and say, "Yes, Lord! May You see my need and invite me to a quiet place to rest and eat, amen." Wouldn't that be wonderful? Isn't that the unspoken prayer request of every momma's heart? *Please, Jesus, I love these people, but I could use a moment of solitude.*

The truth is, as the disciples traveled by boat with Jesus to that quiet place, the crowds followed them. As I imagine the joy they felt as the Lord called them to a place to rest, I can equally imagine the disappointment they experienced when they arrived at their getaway spot only to find more people waiting, full of needs. Can you imagine that? If this isn't the picture of a mother's life in Scripture!

Mark's Gospel records that Jesus taught these people many things, but the disciples noticed another need. They were hungry! So they went to Jesus.

> "This is a remote place," they said, "and it's already very late. Send the people away so that they can go to the surrounding countryside and villages and buy themselves something to eat."
>
> But he answered, "You give them something to eat."
>
> MARK 6:35-37

So He had the disciples gather the food that was available, and He supernaturally multiplied it. Five loaves of bread and two fish miraculously fed five thousand people. God multiplied something else in that moment—strength.

My friend, when taking a break isn't an option, you and I can rest knowing that we are working alongside the Lord. And He is in the business of taking small amounts of whatever we offer Him and supernaturally multiplying it. So tonight we are praying for you. He gave you this family, and He is working alongside you to meet all their needs. He knows that you love them but you are weary.

Tonight we pray for the momma *who has nothing left to give. Lord, she has reached the end of the day and is staring at all there is left to do. She doesn't know where the strength to finish will come from. She's tired and she needs Your help. But, Lord, You are the God of hope. You are the One who makes her heart new every morning, and when her strength runs out, You remind her that Yours does not. Whatever she has to face the rest of this week, this month, or this year, you'll face it together. Please help her rest tonight.*

We ask in Jesus's name, amen.

Jesus, give me strength and multiply my rest as I . . .

_____

_____

_____

_____

_____

_____

_____

_____

_____

_____

who has questions in her heart

*Put your finger here; see my hands. Reach out your hand
and put it into my side. Stop doubting and believe.*

JOHN 20:27

As a young girl raised Roman Catholic in the sixties, I had a lot
of unanswered questions about God. In my town back then, the
Mass was offered in Latin. I knew the tenets of the Catholic faith,
but I didn't know Christ or His Word for myself.

My parents kept a large Catholic Bible on the dresser in their
bedroom, but we weren't permitted to read from it as children. I
would often sneak in and look through it, hoping to find answers
to my questions and the God behind my faith. It wasn't until I was
twelve that I received my first Bible that I could search through

myself. God revealed Himself to me in the Scriptures, and I'm so glad that He has continued to answer my curiosities and hard questions. This is His heart toward us. He offers us wisdom and understanding when our faith feels unsteady.

We see a moment in Scripture when Jesus showed us that He doesn't pull back from our questions but offers us an opportunity to have faith.

After our Lord's resurrection, Jesus appeared to various members of His inner circle. The disciples were hiding together when He was suddenly in the room with them. Well, everyone was there except Thomas.

When Thomas returned, the other disciples began to tell him about the Lord's appearance to them. Thomas wasn't so sure. He said, "Unless I see the nail marks in his hands and put my finger where the nails were, and put my hand into his side, I will not believe" (John 20:25).

When you think about it, the story that the disciples were telling Thomas did seem impossible considering the extent of the injuries that Jesus had sustained during the Crucifixion. We know that Thomas was aware of the nails that had been driven through Jesus's hands and the piercing of His side with a spear because he specifically mentioned those two events to his fellow disciples. But how Jesus loved Thomas!

Here is more of the story:

A week later his disciples were in the house again, and Thomas was with them. Though the doors were locked, Jesus came and stood among them and said, "Peace be with you!" Then he said to Thomas, "Put your finger here; see my hands. Reach out your hand and put it into my side. Stop doubting and believe."

JOHN 20:26-27

The Lord loved Thomas so much that He appeared to the disciples a second time just to give him a chance to believe that He had been resurrected. I love how He specifically offered Thomas the opportunity to resolve his doubts so that his faith might grow.

Church tradition holds that after the Day of Pentecost, Thomas brought the gospel all the way to the coast of India, preaching to many as he traveled. Ultimately, he was martyred there by being speared. How interesting that after Thomas had verified Christ's resurrection by placing his hand where the spear had pierced Jesus's side, he was so committed to his Lord that he could face his own spear without losing his firm belief in the gospel.

Momma, the Lord doesn't mind your questions! He already knows that you have them. He just wants you to take them to Him so that He might settle them for you. Then you can believe, and your faith can be complete! Tonight we pray that every question you have will be answered so that your faith will rest on a firm foundation.

Tonight we pray for the momma *who has questions in her heart. Lord, she might be asking what to do next. She may be wondering why things are the way they are. Perhaps she even needs to know when to move or act or let go. Lord, You know all the questions she has, and You have all the answers. We ask that You'd bring her clarity and direction. Give her confidence and courage as she follows you. Most of all, give her peace.*

We ask in Jesus's name, amen.

Lord, please speak to my heart
about this question I bring to You now:

who needs peace like air

Jesus stood up and gave a command to the wind and the water.
He said, "Quiet! Be still!"
Then the wind stopped, and the lake became calm.

MARK 4:39, ERV

WHEN KOLTON, KADENCE, AND JAXTON were very young, I'd take them to our neighborhood park. They loved the merry-go-round, and I'd help position them in the middle so they wouldn't fall off. They'd laugh as I spun them, and when they were done, they always wanted to give Mommy a turn. It didn't take long before I'd holler, "I'm done!"

As the world whipped by on that playground ride, it reminded me of what was taking place in my heart and mind during those early years of motherhood. Life felt like one big storm of swirling thoughts and racing heartbeats. I desperately wanted someone to grab hold of the rail, stop the spinning, and exclaim, "That's it! You can take a break and catch your breath for a minute." I needed peace, but in the middle of the swirl it was hard to focus on my Father's face.

There's a story in Scripture about Jesus's friends being tossed around in a boat as they crossed a lake:

Jesus said to his followers, "Come with me across the lake." So they left the crowd behind and went with Jesus in the boat he was already in. . . . A very bad wind came up on the lake. The waves were coming over the sides and into the boat, and it was almost full of water. Jesus was inside the boat, sleeping with his head on a pillow. The followers went and woke him. They said, "Teacher, don't you care about us? We are going to drown!"

Jesus stood up and gave a command to the wind and the water. He said, "Quiet! Be still!" Then the wind stopped, and the lake became calm.

MARK 4:35-39, ERV

Have you ever prayed for Jesus to speak to the storm in your life or the swirl in your heart? Have you ever felt as if you're spinning on this merry-go-round of motherhood, and you're convinced God must be sleeping, or surely, He'd have slowed the madness by now?

Let me remind you of this truth before you sleep: Just as the Lord called the disciples into the boat He was already in, He called you into motherhood, knowing you'd find Him there. You're not alone in this. If it's His boat, you can be confident that it will make it to the other side. You can be confident that His peace is traveling with you. If you need Him, you can come to Him and ask Him to calm the chaos in your heart. You can ask Him to bring peace to any consuming fear you feel. And then? You can follow His lead and join Him in finding rest even among the swirl and the storm.

Tonight we pray for the momma *who needs peace like she needs air. She needs peace in her heart, mind, and home. She needs You to settle every racing thought, every troubled relationship, and every area of uncertainty. Tonight we ask that You walk into the room with her and speak to every storm swirling around her and within her. Speak peace to her heart. Speak peace over her home. Just as You told the winds and waves to be calm and they obeyed, You still speak peace to our lives. Bless her tonight.*

We ask in Jesus's name, amen.

Jesus, Your disciples saw You quiet swirling seas.
Now I ask You to enable me to rest
as You calm this storm in me:

who does it all without applause

You are the God who sees me.

GENESIS 16:13

My momma sent me a text message two nights before Thanksgiving. There were no words, just a photo of a digital ear thermometer that showed 101.2 degrees. It was more than a fever. At that moment, I knew all of our Thanksgiving plans would need to change. Like many families, Jared and I spend the holidays with both sides of our family. This year, we'd planned to spend Thanksgiving Day with Jared's family and have dinner with my parents on Friday night. There was one more problem.

Momma's fever didn't just mean we'd need to postpone the

gathering for my side of the family; I had been with my mom only hours before she started showing symptoms of what we learned later was influenza A. I had been exposed and didn't want to take the virus to Jared's relatives. So Jared and I decided to stay home and cancel our Thanksgiving plans altogether. A weekend that was supposed to go one way was turning out very differently than we'd expected, but we had made the right decision. Jared woke up on Thanksgiving morning not feeling well, and that meant if my kids were going to have a Thanksgiving meal at all, I'd have to prepare it alone.

While the kids played and Jared slept, I cooked our family a beautiful dinner. Turkey, dressing, sweet potatoes, mashed potatoes and gravy, green bean casserole, and cranberry sauce were all on the table that night. I stood alone in the kitchen for five hours, chopping, prepping, washing dishes, stirring sauces, checking casseroles, and timing the turkey.

And do you know what happened when it was time to gather and eat? No congratulations banner dropped from the ceiling, no confetti popped from cannons, and no streamers flew across the kitchen. Jared and I sat with the kids and ate a delicious meal together while taking turns saying all the things we were thankful for that night.

I chuckled to myself later that my kids hadn't realized how much work it had been for me that day. They wouldn't understand until they were grown with families of their own just how much effort it had taken for their momma to make that meal alone. Perhaps as they stand in their own kitchens someday, a brief thought will cross their minds: *I bet that was a lot of work for Mom.*

We don't do it for the applause, do we, Momma? We do it because we love our kids no matter their ages. We do it because we are the ones who make the memories, create the moments, and care when often no one else does.

My friend, beyond what our children notice, we can be confident that our Father in heaven sees everything we do. One momma named Hagar, the servant of Abram's wife, Sarai, declared this truth. Pregnant and alone after running away from her mistress, Hagar was sitting in the wilderness when God came and spoke directly to her. She responded, "You are the God who sees me."

He sees you, too. You aren't overlooked, abandoned, or forgotten. You are seen, remembered, and loved. And tonight heaven is cheering you on.

Tonight we pray for the momma *who does it all without applause. Lord, there are no cheering fans for dishwashing, folding laundry, driving carpool, cooking, cleaning, or holding down a job. She does all this because she loves her family. They are her greatest reward and achievement. They are her greatest responsibility and her greatest joy. Lord, tonight we pray for strength and peace as she rests, takes care of sick children or newborns, or finishes whatever still needs to be done after the children are asleep. We, as a community, are praying for each other tonight and cheering each other on!*

We pray in Jesus's name, amen.

Father, help me hear heaven cheering me on tonight about _____ even if the world has not noticed.

whose mind is full

Teach us to number our days,
that we may gain a heart of wisdom.

PSALM 90:12

EVERY YEAR SINCE 1979, I have purchased a new wall calendar for myself. I'm old enough to remember hanging the calendar near the phone in the kitchen so I could record all my important dates and appointments on it. Today, of course, phones aren't attached to the wall and fewer people hang calendars. Now, we can fit it all in our pockets. I take my phone—and the calendar app that comes with it—wherever I go. But honestly, I rely most heavily on something far superior—my running mental list.

That's right. Despite all the advancements of modern technology, there is one form of record keeping that has yet to be surpassed: Momma's memory! When did my child take their last dose of medicine? Momma remembers! When is picture day? Momma knows. Need a science-fair project for school on Tuesday? Momma's on it! Have an orthodontist appointment next month at 4:40 p.m.? Momma has it in her data bank! You need your softball helmet for the next away game, but you left it at Gram's house? No worries! Momma will have it picked up, polished, and ready for the batter's box before school gets out at three.

We remember just about everything, but all of this can take a toll on a momma's peace! What if she forgets something important? What if she tries her best, consults her calendar, and still lets someone down? Plus, there aren't just dates to remember; there are decisions to make along the way. My friend, just as we use tools to help us manage our times and places, we need to lean on the Lord's wisdom to help us make wise decisions.

As Moses prays, "Teach us to number our days, that we may gain a heart of wisdom." Numbering our days means looking at what God has done in the past so we can trust He will meet us in our present and future. As we begin to see the pattern of who God is in our lives—His goodness, His kindness, and His knowledge— we draw on His wisdom as we consider every upcoming event, whether it's written down on our calendar or stored only in our hearts and minds.

So tonight we remind you of Paul's words to his friends in Philippi: "Tell God what you need, and thank him for all he has done. Then you will experience God's peace, which exceeds anything we can understand. His peace will guard your hearts and minds as you live in Christ Jesus" (Philippians 4:6-7, NLT). How encouraging to know that when both our calendars and our minds are full, we can trust that the Lord never runs out of space or wisdom.

Tonight we pray for the momma *whose mind is full. Lord, she keeps all the details for all her people. She knows dates, times, schedules, and preferences—everything from who likes what to eat to who has which practice when. Her mind rarely rests because she is always looking ahead, always making plans to keep her family healthy and happy. Tonight, Lord, we ask for a special kind of rest. Please put her mind at ease so she can have mental and emotional peace. Help her trust You with all her tomorrows.*

We ask in Jesus's name, amen.

Father, please help me track these details
that I am so worried I might forget:

who trusts the Lord

Even if he does not, we want you to know,
Your Majesty, that we will not serve your gods
or worship the image of gold you have set up.

DANIEL 3:18

IT WAS FIVE O'CLOCK ON A FRIDAY EVENING, and vacation Bible school had just ended for the week. As the Christian education director, I'd started with a vision to build a beach in our downtown church's playground. The church had just completed the construction of an outdoor play gym in the shape of a boat. I had thought a beach theme with dump-truck loads of sand, beach balls, and Hawaiian leis would be fun.

VBS had been a huge undertaking but a huge success. So many children grew in their relationship with the Lord while having a lot of fun. I still hear stories from those who attended the program that summer.

Now that the week was over, I was exhausted and ready for a break. I didn't know how long of a break I was about to get. When I met with the church oversight committee a few days later, I was told that—despite the success of that summer session—the church had other plans for future programs that did not include me in the role of Christian education director. Just like that, what I'd thought was secure was gone.

I need to say this: Churches, like families, can be messy. It's important for us to remember that. It can be hard to trust the Lord when the people who represent Him have let us down.

In the book of Daniel, we read about three young Hebrew men who were taken into captivity in the land of Babylon under King Nebuchadnezzar. Do you know this story? By command of the king, everyone was to bow down before a golden idol. But these three men, Shadrach, Meshach, and Abednego, refused. They trusted the Lord, even though the punishment for refusing to worship the idol was death. They told the king, "If we are thrown into the blazing furnace, the God we serve is able to deliver us from it, and he will deliver us from Your Majesty's hand. But even if he does not, we want you to know, Your Majesty, that we will not serve your gods or worship the image of gold you have set up" (Daniel 3:17-18). They were cast into a fiery furnace. King Nebuchadnezzar was startled to see a fourth man in the fire. He called to the three men, who walked out of the flames without even the smell of smoke on their clothes.

Momma, you can trust God. You can trust Him even when you can't trust His people. You can trust Him even when you can't trust the bank balance. You can trust Him even when you can't trust the doctor's report or the school's assessment of your child or the friends in your circle. You can trust Him even when you have lost trust with your spouse or family member. You can trust Him, knowing that He can deliver you from the flames— even if you feel heat around you, He can protect you from being singed. The Lord is walking with you through every trial you're facing. You are not alone! May you come through free and unbound.

Tonight we pray for the momma *who trusts the Lord. She knows that no matter what is happening, she can put her confidence in You. Lord, she trusts You in the storm and in joy. She trusts You when she is struggling and in times of ease and rest. She knows You are good, and she worships You in all seasons. When she closes her eyes to sleep tonight, she will trust You with her tomorrow. Please grant her sweet sleep.*

We ask in Jesus's name, amen.

Lord Jesus, thank You for standing with me
and holding me up as I walk through the fire of . . .

who needs her joy back

Do not grieve, for the joy of the LORD is your strength.

NEHEMIAH 8:10

WHEN OUR KIDS WERE LITTLE, my husband, Jared, built a large sandbox in our backyard. The kids loved digging in it, but they loved getting the hose and flooding it with water even more. Then they could build sandcastles, dig into the cooler sand below, and watch their small tunnels turn into flowing streams.

Just as you might expect a mess after traveling to the beach, our DIY Oklahoma shore came with quite the cleanup. But for some reason, the mess didn't bother me during that time of my life. I was surrounded by disarray anyway. What was a little sand? I was a happy momma who loved to see her children experience wonder at the world around them.

I don't remember setting that version of myself aside, but if I were to fold this season of my life over on that one, you'd find a stark contrast. I got busier, I guess—impatient and easily frustrated. Maybe I just got to the point where life felt too chaotic, and I valued order more than wonder.

The truth is, I don't always feel like the happy momma I want to be for myself or my kids. I wonder if you feel the same way. There's a story found in the book of Nehemiah about the people of God returning to Him. They had been carried away into exile in Babylon. After they were finally permitted to return and rebuild their city in Jerusalem, Nehemiah realized that there weren't any walls to protect the city. So God put it on his heart to oversee the reconstruction of them.

As the people of God returned to the city of God, they heard the Law read to them again. They heard what God had intended for them. They heard how He wanted them to live their lives, and they realized how far they were from what the Lord had for them. And they grieved deeply the difference between where they were and where they wanted to be.

Nehemiah, the governor; Ezra, the priest; and all the Levites answered them:

"This day is holy to the LORD your God. Do not mourn or weep." For all the people had been weeping as they listened to the words of the Law. Nehemiah said, "Go and enjoy choice food and sweet drinks, and send some to those who have nothing prepared. This day is holy to our Lord. Do not grieve, for the joy of the LORD is your strength."

NEHEMIAH 8:9-10

The joy of being with the Lord, knowing the Lord, trusting the Lord, following the Lord, and inviting the Lord into their lives . . . they would experience it. His joy would be their source of strength.

Friend, I think maybe we sometimes get too busy trying to do it all in our own strength. We know we need God's help and try to give it over to Him, but in reality, we just keep doing it ourselves. We end up tired and frustrated, going through the motions rather than experiencing the joy around us.

As we turn our hearts back toward the Lord—confessing that we need Him and rely on Him—we receive Him. And with Him comes joy. Listen, we don't chase joy and get Jesus. We stop and invite Jesus into regular moments like this one. We look around and say, "I can't do it all, and I need You to help me. Help me enjoy my life. Help me enjoy my kids. Take away the burden of frustration that's stealing my joy, and help me remember that You've already figured out all the things I'm worried about." And as He comes into the room, so does the joy of His presence.

Tonight let's ask God to return what may have been lost or stolen by situations or circumstances outside our control. Let's ask God to restore our joy and our strength.

Tonight we pray for the momma *who needs to get her joy back. Lord, she is grateful for the life You have given her, but she isn't always glad. She wishes she could be a more content mom, but when everything feels over-whelming, she doesn't often laugh. Tonight, Lord, we pray that Your joy would become her strength. Please remove all the anxiety, fear, or discouragement that has kept a lid on her laughter. We ask that joy, like a good medicine, would heal her heart from all hopelessness and that tonight she would again have Your supernatural peace and joy.*

We ask in Jesus's name, amen.

Lord, I want to experience Your joy. Help me to rest
in You, even as You work in these areas
of life that seem to be stealing my laughter:

_____

_____

_____

_____

_____

_____

who is mentally, physically, or emotionally exhausted

I have told you these things, so that in me you may have peace.
In this world you will have trouble. But take heart!
I have overcome the world.

JOHN 16:33

Perhaps you are like us. When we are mentally tired, we just shut down. We can't make any more decisions or solve any more problems. When we are physically tired, our bodies ache, and we are sore all over. We cannot do one more load of laundry or wash one more stack of dishes. We have reached the end of our emotional rope, and we are done.

We wish we could somehow prevent those days of exhaustion from happening. We so wish that as Christian mommas, none of us would ever run out of strength, but that's not what God promises us. The truth is that even we Christian women experience times of great burden and struggle. We get tired. We get frustrated. We feel human emotions and navigate imperfect circumstances.

In those moments it is important to remember how much God loves us. His love isn't shown by the absence of struggles. His love is shown by the presence of His Spirit. He does not leave us when times are hard and our difficulties seem to mount. The exact opposite is true.

When writing to the church in Rome, the apostle Paul made a powerful declaration: "Can anything ever separate us from Christ's love? Does it mean he no longer loves us if we have trouble or calamity, or are persecuted, or hungry, or destitute, or in danger, or threatened with death? . . . No, despite all these things, overwhelming victory is ours through Christ, who loved us" (Romans 8:35, 37, NLT). The early church faced these very issues. They lived through the threat of the sword, danger, and famine. They were persecuted and hungry. But Paul reminded them that in the midst of the worst circumstances, nothing could separate them from the love of Christ.

Momma, you may not be facing sword or calamity, but what you're enduring matters to God. Your experience of exhaustion does not indicate the absence of His presence. He is with you even now. Jesus told his friends, "I have told you these things, so that in me you may have peace. In this world you will have trouble. But take heart! I have overcome the world."

Momma, you are loved by the Lord. Let me say that again so that it sinks deep into your heart, mind, and soul: You are loved by the Lord, and nothing can ever separate you from Him.

So when exhaustion comes in any form, lean into Jesus's never-ending love for you. Rest in the truth that "He gives strength to the weary and increases the power of the weak" (Isaiah 40:29). He is with you to help you through every circumstance. He will provide the strength that overcomes exhaustion, and He will give you power to overcome your weaknesses. Let us pray and believe for His presence to strengthen us tonight.

Tonight we pray for the momma *who is mentally, physically, or emotionally exhausted. Lord, You have seen all she has been carrying. You've seen each faithful step she has taken, and You've walked through her days with her. That means You know what her heart needs tonight before we even ask You for it. Whether it's a good night of sleep or just time to relax, You know what will help her. Meet her in this moment and bring her peace.*

We ask in Jesus's name, amen.

Jesus, help me to take heart, knowing You love me and will provide the strength and stamina I need tomorrow to . . .

_____

_____

_____

_____

who wonders how she is going to get through this situation

His followers took him by night and
lowered him in a basket through an opening in the wall.

ACTS 9:25

IN THE SUMMER OF 1977, I went on a mission trip to the island of Haiti. The conditions were pretty rough, but I was making it just fine—that is, until we were told that we had to go by boat over to a smaller island, where we would preach the gospel for a few days.

On the day of our departure, we boarded a small vessel that had no cover but did have a little place in the back where I could sit. The ocean was very rough, and I became seasick almost immediately. The waves tossed the little boat, and it was just too much for me to handle at that time, but there was no turning back. Onward we went.

Once we arrived, we stayed in a very primitive cabin with no beds, so I slept on the dirt floor with my blankets. After we were there a couple of days, I started thinking about the ocean trip back to the main island.

I was sitting on the cabin's little porch, enjoying a cool afternoon breeze while praying about the upcoming ride over the ocean. I asked the Lord to help me because I didn't know how I was going to get through it. Finally, I reached this conclusion: *If only I had some motion sickness pills, I think I could get back okay.*

No sooner had I prayed this than a tall blonde woman walked up the dirt path in front of the porch. She asked what I was doing on the island, so I explained that we were preaching in the local church. I told her I had been so sick on the way here that I'd just been praying and telling the Lord I wished I had some motion sickness pills for the journey home. She reached in her pocket and pulled out two little packets of motion sickness pills. She put them on the porch rail, smiled kindly, said her goodbyes, and left.

I was in the remotest place on earth and needed something I was positive wasn't available for hundreds of miles. But as soon as I prayed, the Lord miraculously supplied exactly what I needed. Do you suppose that woman was an angel?

In the book of Acts, the apostle Paul was also in a desperate situation. He had found out about a plot to kill him. His enemies were watching the city gates for their opportunity. But Acts 9:25 tells us: "His followers took him by night and lowered him in a basket through an opening in the wall."

In other words, the Lord made a way of escape for Paul—an opening he could get through to continue on his journey toward his destiny. Momma, I don't know what your insurmountable situation is, but I do know that God is able to make a way of escape. He knows exactly what you need before you even tell Him. Tonight let's ask Him for what we need.

Tonight we pray for the momma *who wonders how she is going to get through this situation. It feels overwhelming. It feels bigger than she is. Sometimes she feels as if she is down and can't get back up. Tonight, Lord, we see Your hand reaching down to pull her up. You are with her. You will protect and shield her heart. You will help her overcome every situation.*

We believe because we ask in Jesus's name, amen.

Father, please show me the way through this situation that seems beyond my ability to endure:

who loves her momma tribe

He took her by the hand and helped her to her feet. Then he called
for the believers, especially the widows, and presented her to them alive.

ACTS 9:41

EVERY MOMMA TRIBE looks different and forms to meet different
needs. Some are made up of young mommas who are just starting
to raise their children and gather for community and friendship.
Some momma tribes form at church and grow through the Word.
Others, like the one I was in, form in our neighborhoods. When
my daughters were in grade school, the moms on our street all took
care of the kids in our neighborhood, making them lunches and
providing snacks at one house or the other for several years. I still
think fondly of those simpler times and those wonderful women
who were my closest friends.

A very short story in the Bible tells about a group of women who came together to mourn the loss of one of their own, a woman named Tabitha (or Dorcas). Scripture records that she was always doing good and helping the poor. When she became sick and passed away, those who knew her went to get Peter at a neighboring town, where he was healing the sick.

When Peter came into the room where Tabitha's body lay, the women who had been part of her tribe were gathered around her, mourning. They showed Peter the robes and tunics that she had made when she was still with them. I imagine them holding out their arms to show how they proudly wore the clothing sewn in love for each of them.

After seeing the love these women had for their dear friend, Peter asked them to leave for a moment. He knelt to pray and then "turning toward the dead woman, he said, 'Tabitha, get up.' She opened her eyes, and seeing Peter she sat up. He took her by the hand and helped her to her feet. Then he called for the believers, especially the widows, and presented her to them alive" (Acts 9:40-41).

Tabitha was back, and what a sight to find her tribe, once there to mourn, now standing together and rejoicing! It was a wonderful miracle that led many to believe in the Lord.

Momma, you may not have found your own tribe yet. You may be searching for that special group of close friends whom you can count on through thick and thin. But know this: You can be the

Tabitha who covers others with your prayers and gathers friends together in the name of the Lord.

Tonight we pray for the momma *who loves her momma tribe! Lord, they are the most supportive group of friends, sisters, cousins, or maybe workmates. They are loving and caring, and they watch out for each other. They lift her up when she is down. They dry her tears, and together this band of mommas laugh until they cry. They keep no record of wrong. They are the best! Lord, bless each one in this tribe tonight. Grant them sweet, restorative sleep.*

We ask in Jesus's name, amen.

Jesus, thank You for these special women who have come alongside me—whether now or in the past:

_____

_____

_____

_____

who is so stressed she can't think straight

Peace I leave with you; my peace I give to you. Not as the world gives do I give to you. Let not your hearts be troubled, neither let them be afraid.

JOHN 14:27, ESV

"PLEASE PUT YOUR SHOES into the sink and your dishes in the closet! I won't ask again." My tone was far from patient, and the confusion of my words matched the chaos in my heart. My kids knew what I meant and carried out the understood assignments, but they were feeling the same stress I was.

We had just moved to our fifth house in five years, and we were all ready to be settled. Boxes lined the walls, paint rollers from our first DIY projects in the new space were scattered about, and school was starting in less than a week.

I kept telling myself that if I could get unpacked, we'd have peace. If I could finish my projects, we'd have peace. If I could get the kids to school, my home office set up, and my daily life reestablished, we'd all have peace. I had a good goal. My aim was to find the peace we all craved so deeply. But I was pushing us all toward an ever-moving finish line, convinced that a sense of rest could come only when everything was done.

Maybe you've felt the same way. The circumstances that led to your stress may have been different from mine, but perhaps you, too, assumed your peace was dependent on the outcome of your situation. Your anxiety spilled onto those around you, and your pushing actually pulled your family away from peace rather than rushing them toward the rest you all craved.

Every one of us has been in the place where we were so stressed that we couldn't think straight. But there is an important truth we can remember in moments like these: God has given us the gift of His Spirit, a constant Helper, who is ready to come to our aid at all times. He gives us peace in the middle of life's unfinished business.

We just need to stop, recenter our hearts on the truth that peace doesn't come only from finished projects but from the finished work of Jesus on the cross. Jesus made a way for us to have access to His Spirit. He made a way for us to pause in the middle of our most stressful days and shout, "Help!" believing our prayers will be heard. My friend, Jesus is the peace, strength, hope, and wisdom we need for the days ahead. And He is ready to bring to your heart and mind the rest that you desperately crave.

Tonight we pray for the momma *who is so stressed that she can't think straight. Lord, help! That has been her prayer for what seems like weeks. She is desperate for You to step in and help her. She needs peace. She needs hope. She needs a minute to gather her thoughts and come up with a strategy. But mostly, Lord, she needs You. She needs Your love to fill her heart and settle every anxious thought. She needs You to remove the tension gripping her body. She needs You to be everything You are. Help her, Lord.*

We ask in Jesus's name, amen.

Jesus, please help me with . . .

_____

_____

_____

_____

_____

_____

_____

who feels like she cannot handle one more thing

Come to me, all you who are weary and burdened, and I will give you rest.
Take my yoke upon you and learn from me, for I am gentle and humble in heart,
and you will find rest for your souls. For my yoke is easy and my burden is light.

MATTHEW 11:28-30

I WONDER IF SHE KNOWS WHO I REALLY AM.

Those words popped into my head as soon as I saw that the PTO president had sent me a text, asking if I would be the room mom for my younger son's class. I just couldn't take on one more thing, and I wanted to be honest about it. In the past, I might have tried to fit it in anyway. I would have hoisted one more thing up onto my shoulders and struggled under the weight of it all. But nearly fifteen years into parenting, I knew my limits and told her no. My actual reply was something along the lines of "I don't have the capacity to add that to my schedule this year. I do appreciate you thinking of me."

Truly, in the past seasons of motherhood, no one would even have thought of me as someone who could handle the extra responsibilities of being the teacher's parent helper. No one would have assumed I'd be helpful in organizing class parties or taking on extra tasks. Why not? Because for most of my early motherhood, being the "hot mess momma" was my local identity.

I could just imagine the thoughts of the teachers as I flew into the building, dropping off one of my kids: *Here comes Becky Thompson. Late as usual.* The truth is, I wanted a different identity. I wanted so badly to have my life in order. But what I lacked in order or preparedness I made up for in grace toward myself. That was one thing I did have control over while so much of my life and mental health was beyond what I could manage.

See, I knew what was taking place outside the view of those around me. My family and close friends knew what we were working through in that season. They knew the pain that wasn't shared publicly, the loss, the struggle. They knew of the sickness and unease of our hearts. Those closest to us knew the full story. I was more than the momma who was struggling, but I needed grace until this season ended. The Lord saw it all and helped us day by day. There is not one thing He can't handle.

Momma, some seasons are just harder than others. Sometimes the challenges that unfold around us come continually one right after another. But the Lord doesn't ask you to hold everything on your own. He offers Himself:

Come to me, all you who are weary and burdened, and I will give you rest. Take my yoke upon you and learn from me, for I am gentle and humble in heart, and you will find rest for your souls. For my yoke is easy and my burden is light.

He has heard your prayer for help, and the Helper, the Holy Spirit, has come. Don't overlook the gift of His strength to carry you through this season and meet each one of your needs.

Tonight we pray for the momma *who feels like she cannot handle one more thing. Lord, her arms are full, her mind is full, and her emotions are overflowing onto everyone around her. She needs a reprieve. Tonight, Lord, You hear her heart crying, "Help!" You listen as she asks that something would give. Lord, You meet her even here. Give her the chance to breathe. Help her find a moment of rest among all the demands. Supply her with exactly what she needs.*

We ask in Jesus's name, amen.

God, thank You for hearing my cries
and giving me strength. Please help me with . . .

_____

_____

_____

whose life just keeps changing

"See, I am the Lord's servant," said Mary.
"May it happen to me as you have said."

LUKE 1:38, CSB

IN THE EARLY EIGHTIES, my husband and I had season tickets to the orchestra in Oklahoma City. When my older daughter was born, I honestly believed that our biggest adjustment as parents would be that we could no longer attend these concerts. What a surprise to find that *everything* changed!

When you became a momma, everything changed in your life as well—didn't it? Whether you came to motherhood by birth, fostering, or adoption, your daily routine, experiences, and relationships all shifted. Can you think of those early days of motherhood and all of the changes you experienced at once?

Mary's motherhood story was far from ordinary. When she became engaged to Joseph, she didn't know that an angel would soon appear and change her life forever.

The angel told Mary that she would give birth to a baby who would be the Son of God. Overwhelmed with the news, she replied, "See, I am the Lord's servant. May it happen to me as you have said." And it did.

Mary's life changed the moment she was told that she was going to carry the Messiah, and her life shifted again in the moment she first held Him in her arms. But the transitions were far from over.

Mary and Joseph received another heavenly visitor, this one announcing a deadly threat from the jealous king Herod. The angel Gabriel warned Joseph: "Get up. . . . Take the child and his mother and escape to Egypt. Stay there until I tell you, for Herod is going to search for the child to kill him" (Matthew 2:13). And in an instant, everything changed again and they were off, fleeing what was familiar and living as refugees in a land far from home.

At first glance, there's not much we can relate to in Mary's story. A few thousand years and a few thousand miles make her experience seem so far removed from today's modern motherhood. Yet Mary's life reveals a theme consistent across every generation. Motherhood means that life constantly changes. It means we live in continual motion and must trust God across each shifting season.

The Messiah's momma teaches us all an important lesson. God

knows every step of our story, and He knows exactly when the changes will come. We can trust Him. May the profession of our faith in God be the same as Mary's: "See, I am the Lord's servant. May it happen to me as you have said." His love is steady. His heart is true. And even when the world around us is in constant motion, God's presence will remain settled in our hearts.

Tonight we pray for the momma *who feels like life just keeps changing. Lord, just when she thinks she has it figured out, a new set of challenges presents itself. She rolls with it, making adjustments where necessary, but she misses consistency. She just wants steadiness. There was a time when she craved adventure, but today she'd just like ordinary and predictable. Lord, help this momma remember that You are her rock and that You never change. She can look to You and count on You in every shifting season. Bless her tonight.*

We ask in Jesus's name, amen.

Jesus, these changes and challenges are keeping me up at night:

_____

_____

_____

_____

who needs to know that you hear her

May the God of Israel grant you what you have asked of him.

1 SAMUEL 1:17

Do you ever wonder whether God has heard you? If so, friend, we can reassure you: God hasn't missed one prayer of your heart. He hears what you don't even whisper to another person. He hears what you haven't told anyone else. How can we be so confident? We remember the story in Scripture about one woman, Hannah, who persisted in prayer.

Every year Hannah went up to the Tabernacle in Shiloh with her husband, Elkanah. She had no children of her own, so this family celebration was a painful experience for Hannah. She was often taunted by Elkanah's other wife, Peninnah.

One year Hannah couldn't even eat because she was so discouraged. Yet she didn't return home and sleep away her sorrow.
She went to God in prayer at the Tabernacle. She told Him,
"Lord Almighty, if you will only look on your servant's misery
and remember me, and not forget your servant but give her a
son, then I will give him to the Lord for all the days of his life"
(1 Samuel 1:11).

She prayed in her heart, and while her lips moved, she spoke
no words aloud. Scripture records that the chief priest, Eli, saw
her and mistook her for being drunk. Hannah answered,

"Not so, my lord. . . . I am a woman who is deeply troubled. . . .
I was pouring out my soul to the Lord. . . . I have been
praying here out of my great anguish and grief."

Eli answered, "Go in peace, and may the God of Israel
grant you what you have asked of him."

She said, "May your servant find favor in your eyes." Then
she went her way and ate something, and her face was no
longer downcast.

1 SAMUEL 1:15-18

Soon after, the Lord gave Hannah a son, and she kept her
promise to give him back to the Lord.

Hannah's story is beautiful and complex. It's full of determination and God's faithfulness. It reminds us that even when we feel

like we haven't been heard, God has been paying attention to the cries of our hearts.

My friend, that one thing you've prayed about for days or weeks or years—the prayer that you feel certain has gone straight past God's ears—has not been lost. He hears you. He cares. Pause for just a moment and let that truth settle into your heart. Jesus heard as you prayed all alone, as you wondered in your heart, as you cried out for His help. And . . . He loves you. Your prayers are heard by a God who cares. You have the attention of Jesus, who loves you so much He took your place on the cross so you'd never again have to wonder if He heard your prayers.

Hold on, Momma. The answers are coming. "May the God of Israel grant you what you have asked of him."

Tonight we pray for the momma *who needs to know that You hear her. Lord, she has cried and prayed and waited with so much hope and patience, but the voice of discouragement has been loud. And tonight she asks herself whether her prayers have reached You. Tonight we ask You to remind this momma that You have heard even the prayers she didn't whisper out loud. You have a plan for her, and it will all unfold in due time. Give this momma peace tonight.*

We ask in Jesus's name, amen.

Lord, I know that you have heard my prayers about
_____. Grant me peace and
greater trust in You as I wait for Your answers.

who figured it out

If any of you lacks wisdom, you should ask God, who gives generously to all without finding fault, and it will be given to you.

JAMES 1:5

WHEN JARED AND I brought Kolton home from the hospital, he was held constantly. Kolton was our first baby and my parents' first grandchild, so during those first few days there was always someone waiting for a turn to love and rock him. But when the visitors left and Jared went back to work, I noticed that Kolton cried whenever I would lay him down in his crib. Even if he was sound asleep with a full tummy and clean diaper, he'd immediately wake up and cry when he was placed flat on his back. Truthfully, I thought all babies would wake easily and cry for their mommas when they were laid down in their bassinet. I believed it was just a newborn thing that he'd eventually outgrow. It didn't even cross my mind that he cried because he had a medical condition that would require years of treatment.

But I figured it out. I observed. I documented. I paid attention to all the little things and the string of events that only I was there to notice. I made calls to doctors and took him to appointments and found methods that helped relieve his discomfort. I read articles online and searched for solutions. The Holy Spirit led me, and following His lead, I learned what I needed to do to help my baby.

As mommas, this is our constant commission. We wake up daily and do our best to decipher what our children need and how best to provide it. This calling never ends. It isn't ever outgrown. It is the forward march of motherhood as we look, listen, and lean into the leading of the Holy Spirit.

The Lord gives us wisdom. He promises to show us what to do next: "If any of you lacks wisdom, you should ask God, who gives generously to all without finding fault, and it will be given to you." My friend, it's not just a good idea to ask for wisdom; it's the best idea to believe that He desires to give it to you generously. It has never just been about your own understanding; it has been about the Lord's continued guidance. With Him, you'll keep figuring it out. So no matter what you're facing tonight, trust this: The God who has led you through all your hardest places is still faithful and true. He will lead you forward.

Tonight we pray for the momma *who figured it out. Lord, she may be facing a challenge right now. She may be wondering what to do or how she's going to get to the other side of where she's currently standing. But, Lord, You have always shown her the way in the past. You have always shown her what to do, even when she didn't realize it was You leading her. We ask You to remind her now that You have the answers she needs. You have the strategy and solution. She can trust that You are leading her. Bring her peace tonight as she trusts You.*

We ask in Jesus's name, amen.

More than just about anything, Father,
I want to be a good momma to _____.
Please give me wisdom as I . . .

_____

_____

_____

_____

_____

_____

who wishes she'd done it differently

For as high as the heavens are above the earth, so great is his love for those who fear him; as far as the east is from the west, so far has he removed our transgressions from us.

PSALM 103:11-12

I WAS LYING IN BED, remembering a conversation I'd had the week before with one of my children. In this mental replay, I was thinking through my words and my tone and how my correction had been received. Rather than improving my kid's behavior by lovingly helping them adjust their thinking, my words had been defeating. As my child's countenance changed, I knew I had gotten it wrong. I just wished I could've gone back and handled things differently.

This feeling isn't foreign to me. I'm sure if we were completely transparent with each other, you'd say it's not foreign to you either. Mom guilt is a real thing. And whether it comes because we wish we had spoken differently, acted differently, or just were a different sort of mom altogether, the weight of regret can be crushing.

The truth is, we have a very real enemy who wants us to live in continual disapproval of ourselves. He wants us to ruminate on all our failures. He points out our shortcomings, not so we can improve, but so that we will get stuck in the past or in situations we cannot change. If we are so focused on what we did wrong or wish we had done differently, then we will see ourselves as bad moms.

But God isn't disappointed in you, my friend. The Holy Spirit gently corrects you and reminds you who you really are—God's beloved child—in order that you might aim to be even better. His words separate you from your failures, not to hide them, but so that you can press on toward tomorrow with hope. He knows there are moments you wish you could change, and He has healing for your hurting heart. If you're struggling with the weight of guilt tonight, think instead of how Jesus paid the ultimate price so that you don't have to live in the shadow of condemnation.

Psalm 103:11-12 reminds us that God's great love for us depends not on our goodness . . . but His. These same verses remind us that God has taken our shortcomings and removed them so far from us that they no longer hold any power over our hearts or minds.

If our Lord died so that we could be free from the burden of our disappointment, let's live like His sacrifice was worth it. We cannot change the past, but we can look to the future, knowing that God's love will meet us there.

Tonight we pray for the momma *who wishes she had done something differently. Lord, the guilt mommas carry in our hearts can be heavy. We replay moments or seasons in our minds. We may look back on our lives and wish that we had made different decisions or handled situations with more care. Tonight, Lord, whatever guilt this momma is carrying, we ask that You'd step in and take this weighty burden off her shoulders. Replace it with the truth that Your love for her doesn't change based on how she views herself. You say she is a good mom because she looks to You even if she didn't always get it right in the past. Give her peace tonight.*

We ask in Jesus's name, amen.

Lord, thank you for freeing me from the weight
I've been carrying about . . .

159

who loves you but is tired

I waited patiently for the Lord;
he inclined to me and heard my cry.

PSALM 40:1, esv

You work so hard. You're in charge of so many issues and details every single day.

I wonder if you've ever felt like that illustration of the mason jar. Have you seen it? The jar appears full with golf balls. It couldn't hold one more; but then marbles are added. The jar seems full of balls and marbles until coffee grounds are poured in. It is surely full, except it can still hold water. Each addition makes us think that the jar is filled to capacity, but it's not. Somehow more can still be added.

I don't know about you, but this seems like a perfect picture of motherhood. Each extra task or duty feels as if it will be the one that means we cannot take on anything else, but somehow we make room for more. Our capacity expands, our hearts expand, but often our emotions feel stretched beyond what we can contain.

You know, I cry most easily when I am tired and overwhelmed. It's as if my heart is out of room, and the tears just spill out. Do you ever need a minute alone without anyone around so you, too, can let out what you've been holding in? Sometimes when we are busy as mommas, we forget to cry out to the Lord instead of just cry.

The psalmist David was no stranger to tears or to being overwhelmed. He cried out to the Lord in exhaustion. He cried out to the Lord when he was afraid. He cried out to the Lord when he needed help. In Psalm 69:3, he said, "I am weary with my crying out; my throat is parched" (ESV). He was in the Middle East, where the climate was often hot and dry, so even his environment impacted his tears. He loved the Lord, but he was tired.

Goodness, that is us, isn't it? I've cried to the Lord, whether or not tears fell from my face, for all the same reasons David did. Momma, when all you can do is cry, the Lord knows exactly what you mean and how to meet your needs. He knows you love Him, but you're tired. He knows you love your family, but you're tired.

In moments like these, remember what David said of the Lord: "You keep track of all my sorrows. You have collected all my tears in your bottle. You have recorded each one in your book" (Psalm 56:8, NLT). The Lord can hold us and our tears. He never grows tired or weary. His jar never overflows.

Tonight we pray for the momma *who loves You but is tired. Lord, she loves her family, but she is tired. She loves all the blessings that cause her to go, go, go without ever stopping, but Lord, she is so, so . . . so tired. Tonight we ask You to do something supernatural, something only You can do. Give her rest—not just for her body, but for her soul and her spirit. Give her rest that resets every depleted, exhausted, and overwhelmed area of her heart. Multiply the sleep she gets tonight. Restore her hope and her strength.*

We ask in Jesus's name, amen.

Lord, I cry out to You.
I feel stretched beyond my capacity by . . .

_____

_____

_____

_____

who puts one foot
in front of the other

Then they returned and prepared spices and fragrant oils.

LUKE 23:56, NKJV

WHEN I (BECKY) WAS YOUNG, Momma had a business selling
boutique shirts for women (moms especially). I would often travel
with her on weekends to the various craft shows and fairs to sell
these shirts. Long before we began a ministry for moms together,
we were finding ways to connect women across generations in their
love for their families.

One of the bestselling shirts in the nineties had an illustration of a minivan with the words, "A mother's love is measured by
the mile." As a young girl, I didn't entirely understand what that
meant. Now, as a mom myself, I understand that if each mile,

step, and moment of love were tallied, a mother's love would be immeasurable.

Though much has changed over the years, women have always been on the go for their family and friends. Consider the women who followed Jesus for much of His ministry. They marveled at His miracles and were transfixed by His teaching. Then one terrible day, they saw Jesus taken away and watched as He was put to death. They observed as His body was taken down and placed into a borrowed tomb. And when they could follow Him no further, "they returned and prepared spices and fragrant oils. And they rested on the Sabbath according to the commandment."

Can you picture these women with me? Sometimes stories from Scripture seem so far removed from our lives that we forget that these women were just like us and the women we know. They had families and friends. They ate and drank and did what needed to be done.

These women were mourning because they loved the Lord. Though many others left Him out of fear or shame as He was dying, these women followed their Jesus all the way to the tomb . . . and then they continued to do what was needed. As they left to prepare the spices for their Lord's body, a customary way to tend to the deceased, they put one foot in front of the other, physically and emotionally. They continued to serve their Lord even though they had experienced trauma. They continued to do what was needed in the midst of their pain and sadness.

Remarkably, even during great grief, they showed up for the One they loved.

It was to these very women that angels first declared the Good News of the resurrection. They saw the empty tomb with their own eyes. They heard the angels exclaim that Jesus wasn't there but had risen! It was to these women that the angels spoke the words of Jesus, reminding them what their Lord Himself had said with His own lips: "The Son of Man must be delivered into the hands of sinful men, and be crucified, and the third day rise again" (Luke 24:7, NKJV; see also Luke 9:22).

And it was to these women that the joy of sharing the truth of Jesus's glorious resurrection was gifted for the first time. With clothes that likely carried the fragrance of burial, they were able to burst through the doors where Jesus's disciples were mourning His death and declare the wonder of His resurrected life. Their feet had taken them down roads they likely never intended to travel, but their lives were full of stories woven throughout with God's presence and power.

Momma, we, too, find Jesus in days of endless going, and days when we absolutely need to rest. The Good News for each of us is that Jesus rose from the dead and made the way for us to have a restored relationship with God so that we never have to take a single step without Him.

Tonight we pray for the momma *who keeps putting one foot in front of the other. Lord, she doesn't know exactly what waits for her at the end of this path, but she knows You are the One who is ordering her steps. She loves You. She trusts You. And more than anything, she just wants to know that it's all going to be okay. Please remind her that she has never taken one step without You near. You are with her even now. Bring peace and strength for the days ahead.*

We ask in Jesus's name, amen.

Jesus, thank You for walking with me through life. Please guide my steps as I . . .

_____

_____

_____

_____

_____

_____

_____

_____

who needs to know
that you have it all under control

He is before all things, and by him all things hold together.

COLOSSIANS 1:17, CSB

CAN I REMIND YOU OF SOMETHING, MOMMA? God is not surprised by this season of your life. He's not surprised by the events that are unfolding around you. There are many things to do and much to prepare, but the Lord has it all under control—even in those moments when things seem to be unraveling.

When He walked the earth, Jesus ordered His life around appointed times and seasons. One of the Jewish feasts that Jesus and His disciples celebrated together was Passover, which reminded them how God spared the lives of His people in Egypt.

Just before Jesus was crucified, it was time to celebrate the

Passover again. Scripture tells us that Jesus eagerly looked forward to eating this meal with His friends because He knew His time with them was short. He knew it wouldn't be long before He went to the cross, but much needed to be done to prepare His disciples. So Jesus gathered Peter and John and gave them instructions:

"Go and make preparations for us to eat the Passover."

"Where do you want us to prepare for it?" they asked.

He replied, "As you enter the city, a man carrying a jar of water will meet you. Follow him to the house that he enters, and say to the owner of the house, 'The Teacher asks: Where is the guest room, where I may eat the Passover with my disciples?' He will show you a large room upstairs, all furnished. Make preparations there."

They left and found things just as Jesus had told them. So they prepared the Passover.

LUKE 22:8-13

These men knew they could trust Jesus. They did exactly as He directed, but they had no idea that the meal they were preparing would be Jesus's last supper. They didn't know that as they were preparing the meal, Judas, one of their friends, was preparing to betray Jesus. They didn't know that in the hours following this dinner, Jesus would be put on trial, sentenced to death, and crucified. They had no idea.

As those events unfolded, many of Jesus's friends felt confused. Wasn't He the promised Savior? How was He going to help them now?

But Jesus had prepared their hearts just as Peter and John had prepared the meal. He told them what was coming in words that their hearts could understand. At one point before going to the cross, He said, "I have much more to say to you, more than you can now bear. But when he, the Spirit of truth, comes, he will guide you into all the truth" (John 16:12-13).

Truly, as with His disciples, it is a gift that Jesus doesn't always tell us what is coming. It is a grace that He doesn't disclose more than we need to know or can handle. But as I think about all you might be facing, I feel compelled to remind you that the same God who led you through every moment leading up to this one will be faithful to lead you through all that is coming next.

Tonight we pray for the momma *who needs to know that You have it all under control. Lord, there are so many changes happening, and she just feels overwhelmed. Tonight, no matter what is trying to remove her peace, please help her give that situation to You. Please remind her that You can carry it all. Help her to find rest tonight during whatever this busy season holds.*

We ask in Jesus's name, amen.

Lord, when I get anxious, help me to place _____ into Your hands, knowing You have it all under control.

who finds joy
in raising her children

Don't be afraid, little flock.
For it gives your Father great happiness to give you the Kingdom.

LUKE 12:32, NLT

I SAT ON THE FLOOR WITH MY BABY BOY and a camcorder. We
didn't have phones for creating videos back then; at least, that
wasn't the device we would have chosen first for high-quality
recording. So with the battery of the camcorder charged, I was
prepared to do everything I could to capture the moment. I
did not want to miss the first time my son crawled. It all felt so
special.

I loved watching him reach each milestone as he discovered the
world in new ways. Sure, I had been warned of how much work
it would be once he could get around on his own. "You don't want

him to crawl yet if you can help it," friends had warned. "You'll never get any rest when you have to start chasing him." And in some ways, they were right. Life was a different kind of speed once my son began to crawl, but it also meant more opportunities for us to explore together. That season, like every one that followed, has been a gift.

Each stage of life, while uniquely wonderful, seems to come with warnings. There are the terrible twos, threenager blues, pre-teens, middle school years, teenage drama. . . . I've been warned about it all from mommas in the middle of each season doing their best to prepare me for what awaits ahead.

But can I be honest? Each season has come with its unique chal-lenges, but it has also brought tremendous joy. I've felt both frustra-tion and laughter, pain and healing, hopelessness and happiness. It's the beauty of being called to love our children just as our heavenly Father loves us.

So—just in case no one has reminded you today: All that love you feel for your own children? It doesn't compare to the boundless love of God toward you. He cherishes you. He enjoys you. He cele-brates you. As Jesus said, "Don't be afraid, little flock. For it gives your Father great happiness to give you the Kingdom."

God has given us the greatest example of how to delight in our children. Tonight we pray that you feel His admiration and affec-tion for you.

Tonight we pray for the momma *who finds joy in raising her children. Lord, some days are hard, but she looks for the joyful moments. She celebrates the victories both big and small. She loves the simple parts of being a momma. There are moments when her heart is so full of love for her kids that it overflows into smiles and laughter. Lord, please help her to remember that in the midst of all the trouble in this world, her children are among her greatest joys.*

We ask in Jesus's name, amen.

Father, as I consider how much joy my kids
have brought to my life, I thank You for . . .

who can't sleep

In peace I will lie down and sleep, for you alone,
Lord, make me dwell in safety.

PSALM 4:8

Let's be honest. There are morning people and there are night-time people, and they are like creatures from different planets. That's Mark and I. I'm a night owl. The big, bright object in the sky is just an annoyance to me until about 10 a.m., when I actually start to mentally wake up. I am so grateful that my husband is a morning person because those years of getting the kids to school were just brutal. But I love the quiet nighttime hours when I can read, reflect, and mostly just pray.

The Midnight Mom Devotional Facebook page began because a few thousand mommas told us, "Hey, I can't sleep either, and I will pray with you!" In the beginning we called it the Midnight Mom check-in. We'd ask mommas to tell us in the comments of a post where they were and why they were awake. Thousands of women would reply. Mommas had all kinds of reasons for being up late—everything from feeding newborns to caring for sick children, from waiting for teenagers to come home to working the night shift.

Becky and I, who continue to call ourselves night owls, birthed an entire ministry as a result. We posted a nightly prayer, and women responded with their requests for years. Then one night in 2017, we posted a prayer that went viral (see page 54). Tens of thousands of women responded and shared it with the other mommas in their lives. The growth of the page hasn't stopped since. Whether women are naturally night owls or early birds, sleep still remains elusive for so many reasons.

When I was in college, I found a Scripture that I hung on to whenever I couldn't sleep because of worry: "In peace I will lie down and sleep, for you alone, LORD, make me dwell in safety." Knowing that the Lord was keeping me safe while I slept was a new concept to me. For some reason, I thought He was busy only with people who were awake and making significant decisions. But that Scripture helped me know that He is watching over me all the time and that it is okay to rest because He never slumbers.

Tonight, no matter what is stealing your sleep or your peace, remember that God keeps you and those you love in His hands, even after you close your eyes. He will continue to sort it all out, even as you sleep. Our prayer is that He brings you rest.

Tonight we pray for the momma *who can't sleep. She is so tired, but there is so much on her mind and it just won't turn off so she can rest. Lord, tonight we ask that You quiet her heart. Let her rest in the knowledge that You are already working on everything she has to do tomorrow. Let her receive sweet, restorative sleep. Multiply the rest she gets tonight.*

We ask in Jesus's name, amen.

Lord, thank You for meeting me and
helping me in these midnight moments with . . .

who is trying to find answers but doesn't know the question

Nicodemus answered and said to Him,
"How can these things be?"

JOHN 3:9, NKJV

WHEN ONE OF OUR CHILDREN FACED a perplexing medical condition, Jared and I looked for answers everywhere. I took our child to see doctors. I called specialists. I researched online. I found forums for parents dealing with similar symptoms. Despite all my efforts, I couldn't seem to get to the bottom of what was going on. I was just trying to help our child, but I didn't even fully understand what needed to be done. That's when I realized I wasn't even sure I knew the right questions to ask.

Can you relate? Maybe you haven't searched for medical help for your child, but perhaps you have gone through another uncertain situation. Maybe you've searched for answers about your own health, your husband's health, or a parent's health. Maybe you've sought answers about schooling, work, moving, friends, relationships, or extended family. Maybe you're wondering what to do next, where to go next, what this next phase of life is going to look like—but you don't even know exactly what you're hoping for.

Whenever I'm looking for answers but don't even know the right questions to ask, I often think of Nicodemus, a religious leader in Jesus's day. Late one night Nicodemus came to Jesus, asking Him all sorts of questions. As a religious expert, he was supposed to be the one with all the answers, but this man, Jesus, puzzled him. He had heard about the miracles Jesus had performed. He had heard the words that Jesus had spoken. He knew what the ancient Scriptures said about the Messiah. Yet still Nicodemus could not make sense of it all.

So by cover of night, Nicodemus came to Jesus and asked, "How can these things be?" It was as if he was trying to find answers but didn't even fully understand the questions he was asking. Jesus welcomed Nicodemus's questions and told him about the wonderful mystery of God's love. "For God so loved the world that He gave His only begotten Son, that whoever believes in Him should not perish but have everlasting life" (John 3:16, NKJV).

No matter the scenario that perplexes us, we can follow the lead of Nicodemus and come to Jesus with every area of uncertainty. We can trust that He doesn't just know what we are asking, He knows how to best lead us. He knows how to care for us. He knows what our next step is and what the step after that will be as well. If you're in need of answers, let's pause and pray together.

Tonight we pray for the momma *who is trying to find answers when she feels like she doesn't even know the question. Lord, everything in her life may feel topsy-turvy right now. She is trying to find her way through a very unfamiliar situation, and she is struggling tonight. Lord, as a community of praying mommas, we link our arms in prayer for her. We say that You are good and that she can trust in You. Please bless her tonight.*

We ask in Jesus's name, amen.

Jesus, tonight I bring these questions to You:

_____

_____

_____

_____

_____

_____

who is anxious

*Whoever dwells in the shelter of the Most High will rest
in the shadow of the Almighty. I will say of the L*ORD*,
"He is my refuge and my fortress, my God, in whom I trust."*

PSALM 91:1-2

IT WAS THE YEAR 2000, and I was trying out for the cheerleading
team at my new high school. I had always wanted to cheer, but I had
no experience—and in my previous large school, no chance to make
the squad. I walked into the gym for tryouts looking the part. I wore
small black shorts and a tank top, and my hair was pulled up into a
high ponytail. But I didn't know any kick, flip, or cheer that would
qualify me to be on the team, which had won the state tournament
just a few years before. I had, however, skipped the eighth grade,
making me the smallest and easiest high school freshman to toss
into the air. That's what we started with first—stunting.

I was introduced to the girls who would be holding me up in the air as I warily placed my feet—first the right and then the left—into their hands. In unison they called out, "Five, six, seven, eight!" Through each of those counts they guided me into the exact position needed to hoist me up into the air. I was directed to lock my knees, look straight ahead, and let them keep me evenly balanced. I was just to stand there . . . on their hands . . . held above these strangers' heads.

Somehow I was able to complete every attempted stunt despite never having even heard of a Liberty, Arabesque, or Scorpion prior to that day. I was able to single and double down (spin on my way out of the air). I was able to do it all with ease because I just followed instructions and didn't realize there was any real chance of injury. It was all going so well until someone mentioned that I could fall.

Wait! Weren't some of these girls state champs? Their previous success had given me false confidence. So long as I did my part, they would always do theirs. Right? But the moment I realized that even the best girls sometimes get it wrong, everything changed.

While I made the team, cheerleading was no longer something I looked forward to. To be honest, I dreaded every practice, football game, and preparation for the upcoming competitive season. And my stunting showed it. All the stunts I had performed with ease were suddenly impossible. I failed. I fell. And I feared what my inability to shake my anxiety would mean for the rest of the girls.

I wasn't just afraid of getting hurt; I was afraid of letting down my teammates. So I did what needed to be done, but I did it while miserable and afraid.

Momma, I know what it is like to worry that the fear you face daily is going to impact your family. I know what it's like to show up and do what needs to be done despite a racing heart and mind. I know what it is like to struggle through simple things when everyone else seems to face it all with ease. I know you put on a brave face about so much of it.

Friend, you can't fly high enough to come out from the shadow of the Almighty's wings. He is your strong tower, and He won't let you fall. The world may shift beneath you, and life may seem to rest on unsteady ground. But the psalmist reminds us that "whoever dwells in the shelter of the Most High will rest in the shadow of the Almighty. I will say of the LORD, 'He is my refuge and my fortress, my God, in whom I trust.'"

Can you shift your perspective with me for just a moment? You're not being held by trembling hands. You're being held by God Himself. So even when you feel afraid, even when you fear failure or falling, you can trust that the Lord is strong and good. He doesn't fault you for your feelings, but He came to bring hope and healing, His presence and His peace. Tonight let's remember that He is with us and we can trust Him.

Tonight we pray for the momma *who is anxious. Lord, this momma keeps watch over her family. She is constantly on guard. She worries about so much, but oh, how her heart craves peace. Lord, tonight we ask that You'd calm every nerve. Remove all her stress. Help her breathe deeply. Remind her now that You are the One protecting her home and those she loves. You uphold her with Your love. Help her give every care over to You now, and wrap her in a blanket of Your love that brings deep peace.*

We ask in Jesus's name, amen.

Father, I know that You are my stronghold,
and I ask that You hold me fast as I trust You with . . .

whose heart aches

*Now Mary stood outside the tomb crying. As she wept, she bent
over to look into the tomb and saw two angels in white, seated where
Jesus' body had been, one at the head and the other at the foot.*

JOHN 20:11-12

THE PHONE CALL CAME under a clear afternoon sky on a day that
had started out like any other. I, Susan, was told that my seventy-
six-year-old momma, who lived fifteen hundred miles away, was having chest pains and being taken to the hospital. I was concerned, but
this had happened before, and a change in medication usually resolved
the pain. I expected her to be discharged in about forty-eight hours.

A short time later, I received another call saying that her condition had worsened, and they were trying hard to get her stabilized.
I began to pray and intercede. I asked the Lord to heal my mom
and to give the doctors wisdom.

Why hadn't I called her the night before? I had thought about it, but I was so tired. I had things I wanted to tell her. I wanted to hear her voice once more. I just needed extra time, and I begged the Lord for it.

The next call came within the hour. She was gone. The doctors and nurses couldn't save her. I can only remember saying *No!* over and over again as the tears poured down my face.

John 20 tells the story of another woman, Mary Magdalene, who was overcome with grief. She was the first witness to the resurrection of Jesus, but the moments leading up to her encounter with the resurrected Christ are heartbreaking.

She looked into the empty tomb, but instead of finding Jesus, she saw two angels.

They asked her, "Woman, why are you crying?"

"They have taken my Lord away," she said, "and I don't know where they have put him." At this, she turned around and saw Jesus standing there, but she did not realize that it was Jesus.

He asked her, "Woman, why are you crying? Who is it you are looking for?"

Thinking he was the gardener, she said, "Sir, if you have carried him away, tell me where you have put him, and I will get him."

Jesus said to her, "Mary."

JOHN 20:13-16

Mary was the first person to encounter the resurrected Christ. She was the first one to see Jesus after He rose from the dead. But I often think about those moments just before her greatest joy when she experienced her deepest pain.

I think of Mary's confusion, profound grief, and overwhelming sorrow. I think of how her eyes were so clouded with tears that she couldn't recognize Jesus in front of her. And I think about how in an instant, at the mention of her name, she knew it was the Lord standing there.

Momma, in your moments of deep hurt when you weep tears of sorrow, listen carefully for the Lord's voice, no matter what you are suffering or whom you have lost. Jesus is calling your name. He is holding you close. My friend, the empty tomb means hope for all our hurting hearts because it means we will see our loved ones again.

I'll hear my momma's voice again when she says my name, Susan. What a glorious day that will be! But even that will not compare to the sound of my Savior calling my name.

Tonight we pray for the momma *whose heart aches. Lord, there are so many reasons mommas grieve. We grieve the loss of dreams, relationships, jobs, or homes. Lord, we mourn the loss of loved ones or children, those we have held in our arms and those we have held only within us. We grieve when we feel all alone. Lord, You see each momma's heartache. Your arms are big enough to hold her and her grief. Wrap her in Your love right now, and remind her that You never have and never will leave her. Bring her comfort as only You can.*

We ask in Jesus's name, amen.

Jesus, when I can't see You through my tears or
hear You through my cries, I pray specifically
that You would make a way through . . .

who has a strong-willed child

He did what was right in the eyes of the Lord and followed completely the ways of his father David, not turning aside to the right or to the left.

2 KINGS 22:2

I USED TO JOKE THAT if you were to open the dictionary to the word *strong-willed*, you could find a photo of any one of my three children. They know what they want. They follow their hearts. And they don't let anything get in their way. This has made for many interesting stories and moments of motherhood. My kids have pushed back against the boundaries I set for them again and again. And it can be absolutely draining at times.

It's exhausting when a toddler says no and is determined to have things done her way. It's exhausting when a child climbs out of his bed repeatedly night after night, after being tucked in. It's exhausting when a preteen asks *why* over and over and continually challenges every decision because he is convinced he knows better.

But here's the thing. These children aren't pushing against a reed swaying in the wind. They're pushing against their own strong-willed momma who learned a long time ago that God gave me certain attributes for a reason. He made me determined to do all that He placed in my heart, even when others say it is impossible.

Oh, momma friend, so often we need the Lord to remind us of what a gift this can be. We need those with strong determination to do the work of the Lord despite what others may say should be done. We need people who will not bow or bend to the words of men, but who are led by the Word of the Lord alone. We need men and women who know what is right and true in the eyes of the Lord and aren't afraid to say it. We need children who will grow to be adults steadfastly following what God said even if people say it should not be done.

In 2 Kings 22, we find the story of a determined king: "Josiah was eight years old when he became king. . . . He did what was right in the eyes of the LORD and followed completely the ways of his father David, not turning aside to the right or to the left" (2 Kings 22:1-2). Josiah wasn't compared to his natural father, Amon, or his grandfather, Manasseh—both of whom had turned away from the Lord. He was compared to David, the great king who lived generations before him, a man who was strong in his will to follow the Lord.

During Josiah's reign, many people worshiped pagan gods. He had every opportunity to slip into idol worship and the religion of the region, but he didn't. He held fast. He knew what was true, and he didn't waver.

Momma, whether you're just starting out on this journey or you're the momma of a strong-willed adult, the Lord chose you to lead these children. He knew exactly what kind of momma they would need. He knew the kinds of prayers that would need to be prayed for them. And He knew the important role you would play in raising them to be men and women who won't let others sway them from loving the Lord. He is raising up leaders, and you are shaping them today. Praise the Lord for strong-willed children and the mommas trusting Him as they raise them.

Tonight we pray for the momma *who has a strong-willed child. Lord, this one has a mind of their own. She is a fiery daughter. Or he is a determined son. They follow their hearts and don't always think it through to the end. Someday they will make strong, purposeful leaders, but today they are wearing this momma's patience thin. Lord, please give her an extra portion of Your strength. Fill her heart with Your wisdom as she raises these little ones. Help her to rest well tonight.*

We ask in Jesus's name, amen.

Heavenly Father, I pray that You would work in the hearts of my children, _____, so they will serve You wholeheartedly.

191

who is making the best of it

*We fix our eyes not on what is seen, but on what is unseen,
since what is seen is temporary, but what is unseen is eternal.*

2 CORINTHIANS 4:18

I CLIMBED DOWN THE LADDER on my covered patio in the backyard and reached for the next portion of the strand of lights I was
stringing across the ceiling. Then my oldest helped me arrange
comfortable chairs, and my younger two kids helped make a "red
velvet rope" from construction paper to indicate where the line
would form for movie snacks. It was spring 2020, and we were
stuck at home.

With theaters closed, we decided to make our own fun movie
experience. We hung lights. We opened the kitchen window so we
could pretend to purchase soda, popcorn, and other treats from

the concession stand. Then we waited for the sun to go down. That night, in the middle of personal loss, sickness, and sadness, we made an intentional moment for joy and watched a movie on the back patio. That entire season of life was one of tightrope walking the line between discouragement and hope. But we repeatedly asked the Lord to help us make the best of it.

Paul in all of his hardships and sufferings had much to say about the temporary nature of all that we know:

We do not lose heart. Though outwardly we are wasting away, yet inwardly we are being renewed day by day. For our light and momentary troubles are achieving for us an eternal glory that far outweighs them all. So we fix our eyes not on what is seen, but on what is unseen, since what is seen is temporary, but what is unseen is eternal.

2 CORINTHIANS 4:16-18

Momma, you already know that Jesus said, "In this world you will have trouble. But take heart! I have overcome the world" (John 16:33). The truth is, we have an eternal hope that carries us even when life around us seems to be falling apart. We have an eternal hope that someday all these temporary trials and tribulations will pass away. Someday we all will be with Jesus in perfection and there will be no more need to persevere.

It is only in this lifetime that we have the opportunity to praise and worship God even in the middle of struggle or suffering. He can turn mourning into dancing and sadness into joy when we fix our eyes on His presence amidst the problem. What situation do you need to praise Him through today? In what ways can you make the best of any tough situation you face?

Tonight we pray for the momma *who is making the best of it. Lord, it might not be perfect . . . in fact, it might be far from perfect, but it's the best it can be, and she is keeping a positive attitude about it. Well, she's trying her hardest to keep a positive attitude about it. Lord, until it all changes or settles into what it will be, help her to remain hopeful. Help her show her kids how to look on the bright side. Help her cling to the promise of better days ahead. And give her strength to keep putting one foot in front of the other.*

We ask in Jesus's name, amen.

Lord God, as I wait expectantly for Your good plans to be revealed, please give me a mindset that . . .

_____

_____

_____

_____

_____

who needs you to meet her right where she is

From inside the fish Jonah prayed to the LORD his God. He said:
"In my distress I called to the LORD, and he answered me."

JONAH 2:1-2

MARK AND I LIVED IN A QUIET, friendly neighborhood in Oklahoma where it wasn't uncommon to see people out walking their dogs or riding their bikes after dinner. But one summer night, the air had not cooled off even after the sun had been down for a while, so rather than taking a stroll outside, we settled down in the living room to watch TV.

Sometime after nine o'clock, the doorbell rang. I thought maybe it was someone who needed help. I went to the door and looked through the peephole. I saw a large man I didn't recognize.

He was facing the street so I couldn't see his face, but he had his sweatshirt hood pulled up over his head. After looking at Mark, I looked down at the door and realized that the deadbolt (the only lock on the front door) was not secure.

Mark had seen my frightened look and reached the door quickly, snapping the deadbolt into place. As soon as it clicked, the man knew we were home and decided he was coming inside. He didn't need help. We did. The threat wasn't just imagined. It was real.

The stranger kept rattling the doorknob and shouting taunts. For the next ten minutes, Mark reinforced the door by leaning all his weight into it and reassuring me that we would be okay. I called the police, and the man finally gave up and left in a vehicle just before they arrived.

I spent the next few weeks terrified. I became hypervigilant about our safety. I ordered video cameras and extra security. I checked with my neighbors to see if they had any footage of the incident.

I no longer felt safe in my own home. I couldn't sleep at night because every time I closed my eyes, I could hear the banging and the mocking voice on the other side of the door. I needed the Lord to step in and restore my peace. I needed Him to remove my fear and stop this dreadful scene from playing over and over in my mind. My friend, I hope you don't have a similar story of your own.

The book of Jonah tells the familiar story about a man being swallowed by a giant fish after he was tossed overboard from a sailing vessel. God had told Jonah to go to the city of Nineveh to preach repentance to the people there. Jonah did not want to obey the Lord; instead, he took a ship in the opposite direction toward the city of Tarshish. On the way, a great storm arose. The ship was in terrible peril. Finally, the crew threw Jonah overboard, attributing the storm to his disobedience.

After being swallowed, Jonah remained in the belly of the creature for three days before being spit up on shore. If ever a person needed God to meet him where he was, it was Jonah.

I picture him covered in seaweed and floating in the remains of half-digested fish food. I think he may have been bleached white from the salt water and the fish's stomach acid. His skin must have been wrinkled by the constant moisture, and his eyes must have strained to see anything in the darkness as the fish swam at the bottom of the deep. But Jonah didn't lose hope.

"From inside the fish Jonah prayed to the LORD his God. He said: 'In my distress I called to the LORD, and he answered me.'" When Jonah cried out to the Lord, God delivered him out of what seemed like an impossible situation.

Momma, when we feel trapped in overwhelming circumstances, God hears us. Our situations do not change His ability to hear our voice or our hearts. No matter how deep the problem, or how scary the moment, the Lord is with you and will meet you right where you are. You are never alone.

Tonight we pray for the momma *who needs to hear that the Lord will meet her right where she is in this exact moment. Lord, You see everything that is making her situation more difficult, and You are removing each obstacle even now. Lord, please don't let the sound of the enemy cause this momma to retreat from her destiny. Please don't let fear find a foothold in her heart. Strengthen her to keep going. Please help her to keep trying and looking to You. Remind her that You are right beside her. Bless her as she continues forward. She is strong in You.*

In Jesus's name we pray, amen.

Lord, please meet me in this moment with help for this situation:

---

who is worth her own attention

Jesus often withdrew to lonely places and prayed.

LUKE 5:16

I HAVE SAT AND THOUGHT AND SEARCHED and prayed and asked Jesus to help me remember the last time I took time just for myself. And this is the truth I have come to: There isn't one.

I can't point to a girls' trip or a weekend at the spa. I can't point to a time when I shopped a little longer for myself just because. I'm in a season of going and doing and always being the point person. My momma and I also run a worldwide ministry from our living rooms. We have one part-time employee who helps us virtually from out of state. We feel privileged to speak into the lives of so many mommas. Even so, the honest truth remains: Life in this season is nuts.

I can't hop in my car and take off to a vacation spot for a few days on my own. I don't take time for personal beauty treatments or brunches with friends. Once in a while, I stop at the local diner for a Coke in between meetings. Sometimes, friend, that's all the "me time" I get.

Can you relate? Jesus certainly could. Luke reminds us that He "often withdrew to lonely places and prayed." He was continually surrounded by people who needed Him. They needed His healing, His wisdom, and His intervention in the areas they couldn't fix on their own. They needed Him for food, strength, and even peace in the middle of a storm in a sinking boat. They needed Him to be God—and so do you.

We are not the saviors of our story. We are not the saviors of our families. You show Jesus to those you love by pouring out your life with the endless sacrificial love He modeled. But even Jesus knew the importance of withdrawing to be with His Father away from the crowds, and He was God.

Friend, if the Son of God needed to take time to be by Himself to pray, what does that say about us? How much more do we need to separate ourselves from everything and take time to be in His presence? There is nothing wrong with having a spa day or a girls' night out; in fact, those can be so rejuvenating. But true refreshment comes from spending precious time with the Lord, even in the middle of all that's happening around us. We can be alone with Him even when we don't get a physical break from those who need us.

Momma, you are worth taking care of. You are worthy of time to focus on your heart and mind. If no one has offered you this encouragement recently, let me say it: You deserve peace. Let's pray and ask the Lord to help us find space in our busy schedules to breathe.

Tonight we pray for the momma *who needs to remember that she is worth her own attention. There are so many people who count on her. There are so many people whom she cares for. Lord, remind her that in order to care for others, she needs to pour from a full cup. Whisper to her heart that she is worthy of love, joy, peace, and time just for her. Help her find moments to herself, and then meet her in them.*

We ask in Jesus's name, amen.

Father, please help me find time to . . .

who misses the way life was before

One thing I do: Forgetting what is behind and straining toward what is ahead, I press on toward the goal to win the prize for which God has called me heavenward in Christ Jesus.

PHILIPPIANS 3:13-14

RECENTLY WE RELOCATED TO THE SMALL TOWN where my daughter and her family live. We had been planning this move for well over a year. We started packing several months before the moving truck arrived, and even though we had bought a much bigger house, we let many things go that we did not think we would need in our new location.

Leaving our home of seventeen years, where so many friends had come to visit and so many events had taken place, seemed difficult even though we were so looking forward to being closer to family, especially the grandkids.

The first few weeks in this new place were so hard on my heart. I missed my old life—my friends, my routine, just knowing the town and neighborhood I lived in and how to accomplish the daily tasks of coming and going because it was all familiar. One night as we were sitting in our new living room, I turned to my husband and said, "I want to go home!" I felt like a child at camp waiting for the bus to take her back to all that was familiar. I was homesick for my old life. Of course, going "home" to the house we had sold was not an option. This was the place the Lord had given us in this new season, but my heart needed time to process the change.

Momma, there are so many times when you might miss the way life was before now. You might miss what life was like before having a newborn even though you love your little one so much your heart could burst. You might miss what life was like before you had a difficult diagnosis or before a major traumatic event took place in your community. You might miss your children at a younger stage even though the current one is fun and you've looked forward to it for so long.

There are literally dozens of ways life can change in significant ways that cause us to long for what was. It is normal to grieve the loss of the way things were even if you're in a season you prayed for. The important part is not to get so stuck in looking back that you stumble through the present. Keep going!

The apostle Paul told his fellow believers: "One thing I do: Forgetting what is behind and straining toward what is ahead,

I press on toward the goal to win the prize for which God has called me heavenward in Christ Jesus." You are on your way to something really good even if it doesn't feel that way right now. The Lord is making all things new, and the joy of every season is discovering how He will meet you even here . . . even now.

Tonight we pray for the momma *who misses the way life was before. Lord, she looks for the good in things and can see how there is some good in this new season. Even so, she often finds herself missing the way the world was just a few months ago. Will it ever stop feeling so uncertain? Will everything ever settle down and feel less scary? She is overwhelmed and homesick for a life that seems gone. Help this momma tonight. Hold her close. Help her know that good days are ahead and that it will all be okay.*

We ask in Jesus's name, amen.

Jesus, comfort me and lead me as
I trust You with this change in my life:

who is tired of rushing around

Martha, Martha, you are worried and upset about many things,
but one thing is necessary. Mary has made the right choice,
and it will not be taken away from her.

LUKE 10:41-42, csb

When I married Jared, I joined a large family that loves gathering for meals. No matter how big the kitchen, there never seems to be enough room for all the preparation that must be done, and there never seems to be enough space in the oven for all the food. Preparing to cook takes just as long as the actual cooking. And coordinating the timing of the meal is done only by the wisest of the women.

When I read the well-known story about the two sisters, Mary and Martha, in Luke's Gospel, I can hear the pots and pans clanging. I can smell the food cooking and picture Martha with sweat on her brow. As she stirs something in the kitchen, wipes her hands on a cloth, and then rushes to find Mary, I can sense her sigh of frustration. And when she spots her sister sitting at the feet of Jesus, I can see her on the brink of exhausted and overwhelmed tears. I've been her. Maybe not with my sister, but definitely with my own husband and kids.

Don't they care that I'm doing all this work for them? Don't they see how much effort I'm putting into making their lives more enjoyable? Would it hurt them to help out or at least notice? Come on, my friend, don't let me be the only one to admit I've loudly shaken out a new trash bag or slammed the dishwasher door just so my family notices that I'm still going and they're still sitting.

The truth is, when Martha found Mary at Jesus's feet, she didn't ask Mary to get up. She *told* Jesus to tell Mary to get up. Yikes. I've prayed like that before too. I've talked to Jesus and told rather than asked Him what should happen next.

Yet instead of ordering Mary to help with the preparations, Jesus offered Martha the help she really needed. He reminded her that work is good, but it shouldn't take priority over rest in the presence of Jesus.

My friend, I know you rush from one thing to the next. You are constantly on the go. But can this story serve as a quick reminder for the days ahead? Your value isn't determined by what you do or do not get done. I have a feeling you already know that and just might need someone to bring it to the front of your heart. There will be more dishes to wash tomorrow, more errands to run, meals to prepare, clothes to clean, toilets to scrub, bills to pay, problems to solve, and life to live. Don't rush right past rest. Jesus wants to meet with you even in your going. Let's take just a moment and recenter our hearts on what He says is the one thing we really need.

Tonight we pray for the momma *who is tired of rushing around. Lord, it feels like all she ever does is hurry from one place to another, from one task to another, from one crisis to the next. Lord, tonight she needs Your peace to flood her heart. She needs to slow down for a minute and remember that she's a person, too, not just a chauffeur, a housekeeper, or even a crisis manager. Be with this momma tonight as she winds down after another day. Please grant her peace and rest.*

We ask in Jesus's name, amen.

Jesus, in these quiet moments,
help me to sit at your feet and find rest from . . .

who is just over it

"My house will be called a house of prayer,"
but you are making it "a den of robbers."

MATTHEW 21:13

"That's it! I'm done!" Have you ever reached a point where you were just over it? I'm not sure what your "it" is, but maybe you decided you weren't going to listen to it, look at it, or deal with it anymore.

Jesus knew the feeling. There is a moment in the Bible where Jesus went up to the Temple, as He had many times before; but this time the merchants and money changers (the people exchanging currency so worshipers could buy animals to be sacrificed) made Jesus furious.

This trip into Jerusalem was different from Jesus's earlier

visits. He had arrived in the city the day before, on what we now celebrate as Palm Sunday. The people had run before Him, calling out "Hosanna!" and laying tree branches on the road in front of the donkey he rode on. He had made a triumphal entry into the city. But when He reached the Temple, the scene was far from celebratory:

> Jesus entered the temple courts and drove out all who were buying and selling there. He overturned the tables of the money changers and the benches of those selling doves. "It is written," he said to them, "'My house will be called a house of prayer,' but you are making it 'a den of robbers.'"
>
> MATTHEW 21:12-13

This scene is a stark contrast from another occasion in Scripture where Jesus sat with the teachers in the Temple when He was only a boy, causing those who heard Him to be amazed at His understanding. At that time, He had traveled to Jerusalem with His parents for one of the holy feasts. On their journey home, Joseph and Mary realized Jesus wasn't with them. When they frantically returned to Jerusalem, they found Him "in the temple courts, sitting among the teachers, listening to them and asking them questions" (Luke 2:46).

Twenty years later, Jesus was very familiar with all that went on in the Temple. He had seen firsthand the practices of exchanging money and selling doves at exorbitant rates in the house of worship. And this time, He was done with it.

He was about to face a trial, go to the cross, and die as the ultimate sacrifice for His people. So one of His final acts was clearing out the Temple to remind everyone there of the purpose for the house of the Lord.

Momma, there is a way to be over it and not overcome by it. We can be over our frustration and move on to a place of faith. We can be over our anxiety and begin the process of healing and health. We can be over the parts of our lives that seem to be holding us back and move on to our destiny. Jesus was done with the money changers and the sellers in the Temple. So He cleared them out. Then He continued His calling of proclaiming the Good News of the Kingdom and teaching His disciples. Tonight may Jesus's holy discontent compel you to move deeper into your destiny and calling.

Tonight we pray for the momma *who is just over it. Lord, she's over the constant contemplating about what the future will hold. She's over her own frustration and her own anxieties. She's just over them. Lord, tonight we ask that she would draw ever closer to You in these moments. Help her to know that You aren't frustrated with her emotions, that You created us as emotional and intellectual beings with minds, emotions, and wills, and that You understand why she feels this way. Please give this momma peace tonight. Help her wake up with fresh strength.*

We ask in Jesus's name, amen.

Jesus, I am so over _____.
Please help me move past this and into . . .

who is an aunt

God sets the lonely in families.

PSALM 68:6

HAVE YOU HEARD THE POPULAR SAYING that it takes a village to raise a child? My daughter often remarks that in this day and age, the joke is, "I'm still waiting for my village to show up. Do I call them, or do they call me?"

As I was growing up in the sixties in my big Italian family, it took the aunts, the nanas, and the first, second, and third cousins to help raise all the kids. Back then, everyone who wasn't a nana was called "Aunt," even if they were your cousin twice removed or your momma's best friend. If they were a female adult and you were a child, you addressed this person as "Aunt." Each one seemed to have something special to contribute to my life.

There was the aunt who helped me learn to sew, a fantastic gift I have used so many times. Another aunt gifted me with back-to-school shoes that I still think of and am grateful for to this day. I had one aunt who helped me get my first job at a restaurant. My aunts provided guidance, love, and support.

One of the greatest gifts I ever received from an aunt was a Bible and the gospel message. At the time, I did not know that the wonderful story of salvation in the Bible was personal. I had no idea that Jesus's death, burial, and resurrection were for me. It was this aunt who showed me John 3:16: "For God so loved the world that he gave his one and only Son, that whoever believes in him shall not perish but have eternal life." She completely changed my life and is one reason I'm writing this book with my daughter today.

Mommas, we are part of other people's stories. Whether or not you have nieces of your own, you are an "auntie" in someone else's life. You are an "aunt" by birth or by your choice to be part of the village that is helping children become the wonderful people they are destined to be.

Perhaps you don't have a close family, or perhaps you live far away from them. In the Psalms, we read that "God sets the lonely in families." What a beautiful thought! Even the lonely can find close relationships within a family. In other words, those precious relationships can be created right where you are, and the Lord can orchestrate them for you! He loves you so much that He didn't only send His Son for you, He also sent you His family. Tonight let's pause to be grateful for all the "aunts" in our lives.

Tonight we pray for every aunt, *auntie, tia, zia, and great-aunt who makes our children's lives so much richer by being in them. She may be called* _____. *Her love and devotion, care and concern, huge heart and helping hands bring so much fun and joy to us. We are so grateful for her hospitality and help. Lord, remind us of the important role we play as aunts in the lives of those in our community. Help us point others to You, and help us be a blessing.*

We ask in Jesus's name, amen.

Father, thank you for these aunts and special women in my kids' lives:

_____

_____

_____

_____

who needs to know that she's not alone in this

Do not fear, for I am with you; do not be dismayed,
for I am your God. I will strengthen you and help you;
I will uphold you with my righteous right hand.

ISAIAH 41:10

NOT EVERYTHING WE'VE FACED FITS in the tidy lines of printed books. The stories are too raw and jagged. The path veers toward places far too personal to share. These experiences and seasons are surely part of our stories, but they are the chapters reserved for us and the Lord alone to remember.

So, my friend, you'll have to trust us when we tell you that we know what it is like to carry a heavy, unseen burden—one perhaps shared with no one but the Lord. We know what it is like to go through the hard, the heavy, the horrible. We know what it is like to feel misunderstood and unheard. We know what it is like to wake up holding "this" and wondering whether today will be the day God does something about it. We know what it's like to wait for God to shift the things we have been praying about for days, months, or decades.

So without laying out a valley-to-mountaintop tale of exactly how God led us out of those not-so-shareable seasons of life, we will say this: The God who met us will meet you. The God who has taken every step with you up until this moment will walk with you through every one of your coming days. He will lead you to the other side.

Jesus knows what you're facing. He knows what is up ahead. And the One who set the world into motion, the One who knows every beat of your heart and the very cadence of your steps, will keep you moving toward the good plan He has for you. You are not alone. You are far, far from alone.

These words from God are designed to go straight to your own heart: "Do not fear, for I am with you; do not be dismayed, for I am your God. I will strengthen you and help you; I will uphold you with my righteous right hand."

Whatever your "this" may be, you are not alone. He is holding you now.

Tonight we pray for the momma *who needs to know that she's not alone in this. Lord, You know what her "this" is. You know what she is facing, all she is carrying, and what she is walking through right now. She believes You're there, but she can't always hear You. Tonight settle deep within her the truth that she's not alone. You see her and know every detail of her life. You haven't left her and never will. She has You, and she has her best friends holding her up, reminding her that she isn't facing any of it by herself. Bless her tonight. Give her rest.*

We ask in Jesus's name, amen.

Oh, Lord, thank You that You promise to walk with me through every struggle, even those I have shared with no one else. Please remind me tonight that I'm not alone in this:

_____

_____

_____

_____

_____

_____

_____

who is asking why

I cry out to the LORD; I plead for the LORD's mercy.
I pour out my complaints before him and tell him all my troubles.
When I am overwhelmed, you alone know the way I should turn.

PSALM 142:1-3, NLT

HAVING SPENT THREE DECADES IN MINISTRY, I've heard women
cry out to God in many ways. I've heard shouts of adoration and
celebration. I've heard groans of grief and heartache. I've heard
women wail in frustration and anger. I have met women where they
are and wrapped my arms around them, bringing them to the Lord
in prayer as they cry out to Him. The prayers of a woman's heart
are so personal and raw.

The prayers that stayed with me are those from women who see
God differently than I know Him to be. They attribute to God all
the hardship of the broken world we live in rather than see Him

as the rescuer who meets us in our pain. For decades, I have heard women ask God *why*.

So I have to ask you a question: Have you ever experienced so much worry or pain that your own heart and mind couldn't process it? You lived through something tragic or traumatic that made you question the Lord. You wondered whether He was displeased with your doubting heart. You wondered (even if you never told another soul) whether the trial was your own fault.

King David was holed up in a cave and afraid for his life when he cried out to the Lord, "I pour out my complaints before [the Lord] and tell him all my troubles. When I am overwhelmed, you alone know the way I should turn."

The Lord does not fault us for our questions or our weaknesses. He does not hide His face from us in our time of need. He wants us to know Him as a kind and generous Father who made a way for us to never face any of life's trials alone.

Momma, we have all had those days and weeks when the problems just keep coming. But here is a tool to help you not just survive but thrive: Make going to the Lord a priority, especially when life feels overwhelming . . . especially when your heart is asking *why*. In His presence, you will find the answer.

Tonight we pray for the momma *who is asking why. Lord, the anxiety she feels is heavy. She already has a cup overflowing with the "what-ifs" and the "what thens," and now she wonders, Why, Lord? We ask that You bring Your peace to every situation this momma is facing. Help her heart to stop racing and her mind to settle. Help her see where You have been, what You have been doing, and that You're not displeased with her or her questioning heart. Please bring every answer she needs.*

We ask in Jesus's name, amen.

Lord, I look to You for guidance because
You alone know the answers to my questions about . . .

who holds it all together

Who has the wisdom to count the clouds?
Who can tip over the water jars of the heavens?

JOB 38:37

ARE JARED AND I THE ONLY PARENTS who have large plastic bins that hold all the random LEGO pieces from sets that have either fallen apart or been taken apart to make room for new creations? Sometimes these bins get pushed to the back of the closet, and sometimes they are just shoved under the bed. But each one represents hours and hours of playtime, learning, and building time.

The fact is, I am a terrible LEGO builder. For some reason I can't seem to follow the very clear directions, complete with pictures, that come in every box. But my oldest son is amazing at it. When he was five, he built the LEGO version of the *Millennium*

Falcon from Star Wars all by himself. We still marvel at his accomplishment because the set was meant for much older children to assemble.

Even though I am not great at making these creations, I have learned something important: In any build, there are key pieces that hold the whole thing together. They are the linchpins of the entire project. Without them, the entire design will fall apart. Sometimes the project can't even be completed unless those bricks are in place.

Many times we moms feel like those linchpin pieces. It seems that without us, the whole structure would just collapse. We are the only ones who can hold it all together and make it all work correctly. Momma, while you are the guiding force that builds and sustains the rhythm of your household, tonight we offer this simple reminder: The Lord is truly the One who holds everything together.

The book of Job in Scripture describes a man who was terribly afflicted with many trials. In Job 38, the Lord spoke to him out of the whirlwind. All throughout the chapter God reminded Job of His power in creation. "Who has the wisdom to count the clouds? Who can tip over the water jars of the heavens?" In other words, who knows how many clouds there are in the sky, and who can make it rain? The entire chapter showcases the majesty and power of our Creator. Tonight let's lean into the fact that He is the One who upholds all things. Let's trust Him to bring peace and joy to our everyday lives.

You may feel like it's all been up to you, but He has His arms around you and your children. He is able to sustain everything with His powerful Word.

Tonight we pray for the momma *who holds it all together for everyone. Lord, when everyone seems to need her to figure it out or manage the chaos, she does her best. She just keeps going and trying her hardest. She loves her family fiercely, but she is tired. She needs to know that You hold her and her family. Please give her peace and help her rest as she trusts in You.*

We ask in Jesus's name, amen.

Father, let me rest in the knowledge that
You hold me up as I try to hold together . . .

who loves her children but is tired

When he came back, he again found them sleeping,
because their eyes were heavy.

MATTHEW 26:43

I CHECKED MY REARVIEW MIRROR for the third time since pulling out of the store parking lot. Kolton and Kadence were strapped into their car seats behind me. They weren't fighting or being ornery; I was just watching for signs of drowsiness, praying that the gentle hum of the road had not caused my kids to slip into back-seat sleep.

"What do you see outside the window?" I asked Kolton, desperate to keep his eyes open and reserve his full naptime for later. His eyelids were heavy, and to be honest, so were mine. We were about twenty minutes from home, where we could all take a nap.

"Is Sissy still awake?" I asked him. Her car seat was still rear facing, so I couldn't tell if I had lost the battle to the back-seat snooze and would have to put aside all hope of a nap for myself.

Do you remember days like these? Are you in the middle of them now? I would plan my entire schedule around naptimes. I don't know about you, but there are moments when I love my children, but I'm tired. I need a break. I need a nap myself. I need the whole world to pause like one of those movies in which the characters freeze in place and everything just stops.

A few of Jesus's disciples must have felt the need for sleep as well in the moments leading up to His arrest and trial. Jesus took them to a quiet garden that night and asked them to keep watch with Him while He prayed. They loved the Lord, but they were tired too. As Jesus went a little distance from them to pray, these men fell asleep. Three times He returned to ask them to watch and pray, and all three times He found them sleeping. I used to think this said something about their spiritual lives, but now I realize it says they were human like us. They were exhausted, overwhelmed, and just couldn't keep their eyes open.

Momma, no one would doubt their love for the Lord, just as no one would doubt your love for your children. God knows that you don't just need sleep; you need the days ahead to be full of peace.

Tonight we pray for the momma *who loves her children but is tired. Lord, she loves her life, but she's tired. She loves her family and all You've given her, but she's tired. Her heart craves a rest and a reset. She needs more than a good night of sleep. She needs the next steps to be lighter. Tonight, Lord, please do what only You can. Bring her peace and rest. Because she loves her family, she loves You, and she'd really love a minute to breathe. Please supernaturally multiply the rest she receives.*

We ask in Jesus's name, amen.

Lord, grant me peace and rest tonight as I lay my family's needs before You:

_____

_____

_____

_____

_____

_____

_____

who feels discouraged

Then their eyes were opened and they recognized him.

LUKE 24:31

MY FRIEND, SCRIPTURE IS FULL OF PEOPLE just like us—men and women who lived through the hard and heavy, the terrible and trying. They experienced great joy in the presence of Jesus and deep discouragement when they didn't understand where He was or what He was doing.

No wonder, then, that the words of the women who had witnessed Jesus's empty tomb seemed like "idle tales" (Luke 24:11, NKJV) to the ears of the apostles. Mary Magdalene, Joanna, Mary, the mother of James, and others had returned from the empty tomb, declaring that Jesus had risen from the dead. But the disciples wondered how that could possibly be true.

Two followers of Jesus who heard this news set out on a journey toward Emmaus, about seven miles from where the disciples were gathered. As they walked, "they talked together of all these things which had happened" (Luke 24:14, NKJV). But another joined them on their journey.

Jesus Himself drew near and went with them. But their eyes were restrained, so that they did not know Him.

And He said to them, "What kind of conversation is this that you have with one another as you walk and are sad?"

Then the one whose name was Cleopas answered and said to Him, "Are you the only stranger in Jerusalem, and have You not known the things which happened there in these days?

He said to them, "What things?"

So they said to Him, "The things concerning Jesus of Nazareth, who was a Prophet mighty in deed and word before God and all the people, and how the chief priests and our rulers delivered Him to be condemned to death, and crucified Him. But we were hoping that it was He who was going to redeem Israel.

LUKE 24:15-21, NKJV

They continued to walk together, and for the remainder of the seven-mile journey Jesus clearly explained the fulfillment of Scriptures concerning Himself. The two travelers invited Jesus to come in and share a meal with them, but it wasn't until He took bread, blessed it, broke it, and offered it to them that they recognized Him.

Jesus was more than just a tale. His resurrection was real. And they had encountered the risen Lord.

Maybe you feel as confused as these two did on their journey from Jerusalem. Maybe you're in a season where hope itself feels like an idle tale. Maybe you've tried your hardest and done as much as you can, but you wonder how much longer you can believe for better days ahead.

Tonight I'd like to remind you that the Lord is walking with you. Perhaps the stress of your situation has blinded you to even a hint of His close love, but He has been with you all along. It's not hopeless. The stories you have heard of others encountering His love aren't just tall tales. He is with you even now. We are praying that the Lord opens the eyes of your heart to see that He is near to you in this moment.

Tonight we pray for the momma *who feels discouraged. Lord, she has done her best to remain hopeful for the last few months. She has been a rock for her family. She has carried the mental load, making decisions and working out details in so many areas of life. But, tonight, she has run out—it may be that she has run out of patience or hope or joy or strength. Lord, we ask that You breathe new life into her bones. We ask for color to return to the gray areas of her heart. We ask for fresh strength to spring up like flowers from winter soil. We ask for hope. Bless her tonight.*

We ask in Jesus's name, amen.

Jesus, please walk alongside me and reveal
the ways You care about these things I'm facing:

who keeps it together for her family

My grace is all you need. My power works best in weakness.

2 CORINTHIANS 12:9, NLT

CAN I ASK YOU A QUESTION? Who told you that you couldn't fall apart? Was it someone else? Or at some point did you convince yourself that if you began to show others how you really felt, you'd never be able to package your emotions back up? Do you ever view your stress as if it were being held behind a huge dam, with no way for you to let out just a little of the pressure at a time?

So you stay strong. At least, that's the face you put on for your family. That's the way you've resolved to remain resilient.

But can I say something you perhaps desperately need to hear? There are places in your heart that God wants to touch so He can bring healing to them. He knows you need Him. Deep within, you know that only He can help you with all you've been carrying inside for so long. But you're convinced that if you admit you're not okay—if you actually feel your feelings—they will swallow you whole. So you just keep burying them beneath busy. You keep pressing through. But God is asking you to trust Him and to let Him be strong on your behalf.

Sometimes we tell ourselves we need to ask God for help only when we have failed. We have decided that when we can't do something, that's the time we need to call in the reinforcements of heaven. But the truth is, we are *always* in need of heaven's help. When Paul, a great man in Scripture, struggled, he asked the Lord to take away his difficulty. God answered: "My grace is all you need. My power works best in weakness."

My friend, weakness is an invitation to allow God's strength to replace ours. But it requires us to acknowledge that we aren't as strong as we may seem to others. We aren't held together on the inside as much as we may appear to have it together on the outside.

It's okay to feel weak. It's okay to feel scared. It's okay to feel overwhelmed or unsure. It's okay to be a human who needs God's help. You can fall into the arms of a good God who will put you back together better than before. He wants to work through you. Rather than keep it together for our families, let's turn to Christ, who brings true hope and healing, whose power works best in weakness. And let's share Paul's response to Jesus: "So now I am glad to boast about my weaknesses, so that the power of Christ can work through me" (2 Corinthians 12:9, NLT).

Tonight we pray for the momma *who is doing her best to keep it together for her family. Lord, she has tried to control everything (including her emotions), fearing that if she lets go, she will fall apart and everything else around her will too. Tonight help this momma see that You are keeping her together with Your love and Your power. She isn't held together by her own strength, but by Your grace and mercy alone. When she feels like falling apart, she can fall into Your arms, and You will hold her and everything she is feeling. Bring her peace and relief tonight.*

We ask in Jesus's name, amen.

Jesus, You already know what my heart holds.
Tonight please help me with this:

who needs healing

*I am the L*ORD*, who heals you.*

EXODUS 15:26

I STUMBLED OUT OF BED and toward the adjoining bathroom, calling out for Jared as I went. The pain was debilitating, and I couldn't lie down any longer. No position was comfortable. I was in agony and collapsed on the cool tile.

It wasn't the first time I had experienced endometrial pain like this. For years, at the same time each month, I lost days of my life to the disease. Medicines weren't helping. Now doctors were suggesting surgery, though I was still hoping to find another solution. On this night, however, we were smack in the middle of a worldwide health crisis. Just going to the emergency room felt dangerous, but it had to be done. I called out to my husband from the bathroom floor, and he drove me to the hospital.

I was sick at a time when the whole world seemed to be sick too. It was scary on so many levels, which only added to my anxiety and stress. Finally, I was able to see a doctor I trusted, and almost two years later I had surgery that brought relief.

Momma, sickness changes every rhythm in our homes. If we are the ones who are ill, others might need to come and help. If our children are the ones who are sick, we add their care to every other duty that we have. If a loved one or family member is sick, we may not be able to be with them, but caring about them can add mental stress to our already full minds. The need for healing is persistent and loud.

The good news is that God says this about Himself: "I am the LORD, who heals you." We might think of God's healing as always coming in an instant, but sometimes that healing is a process.

In the Bible, an army commander named Naaman suffered from leprosy. Though initially skeptical about the prophet Elisha's instructions, he obeyed: "He went down and dipped himself in the Jordan seven times, as the man of God had told him, and his flesh was restored and became clean like that of a young boy" (2 Kings 5:14).

Jesus once healed a blind man in stages. He touched the man, who glanced around and said, "I see people; they look like trees walking around" (Mark 8:24). But Jesus wasn't done. "Once more Jesus put his hands on the man's eyes. Then his eyes were opened, his sight was restored, and he saw everything clearly" (Mark 8:25).

Momma, healing is available to you and to those you love, and it can come in so many ways. Whatever healing you are praying for tonight, no matter how long you've faced this sickness or disease, we are praying and believing with you for the Lord to do what only He can.

Tonight we pray for the momma *who needs healing. Lord, she may need physical healing, emotional healing, or healing from trauma and stress. Lord, her body, her mind, and her heart need restoration; and together we cry out to You for mercy. Lord, please give her Your healing grace. We thank You so much. Please give this momma rest.*

We ask in Jesus's name, amen.

Oh God, my Healer, You alone know the pain
I feel tonight. Please comfort me and deliver
me from this physical or emotional pain:

who is going through a transition

There is a time for everything, and
a season for every activity under the heavens.

ECCLESIASTES 3:1

TRANSITIONS CAN BE HARD. The change from what we have known to the unknown can be really upsetting to our minds and our emotions. Even if it is a transition that is expected and hoped for, the actual event can be quite difficult because there are so many adjustments.

After spending months helping plan Becky's beautiful wedding, it struck me that she would not be coming home afterward like she had during her college days. The transition to empty nester made me very sad even though I already loved her new husband like a son.

The truth is, transitions—even those that come from the very happiest of circumstances—can still be hard or heavy.

Momma, the Bible tells us that "there is a time for everything, and a season for every activity under the heavens." This means that there is a time for our transitions!

The Old Testament was written by Hebrew authors. Their thoughts about time were much different from our Western ideas. We think of time as linear—we go from point A to point B, and the goal is always to move forward.

But the Hebrews' view of time was circular. The cycle of the earth going around the sun and the moon going around the earth are great examples of seasonal thinking. Why is this helpful information? Because thinking like people in the Old Testament enables us to see that change may be uncomfortable, but it's a constant in our lives. It's the way God created the earth and the universe. It's the way He set a circular rhythm of life and seasons as part of His plan.

So as we pray for you, Momma, in whatever transition you're going through tonight, remember that you have already successfully navigated many seasons in the past and will go through many more in the future. God sees and directs them all.

Tonight we pray for the momma *who is going through a transition. Lord, this momma didn't feel ready. Maybe her baby is going to school or to college. Maybe she is going back to work or coming home after years in her career. Maybe she is making a big decision that impacts everything, and it's all new! Lord, You are God on both sides of the sea. You are the God before this transition and the God after. You have led her all this way. Hold her close to You as she processes this big change and comfort her as only You can.*

We ask in Jesus's name, amen.

Lord, hold me close and remind me that
You are the God who never changes or
leaves me as I navigate this transition through . . .

who has a newborn baby

Because you are my help, I sing in the shadow of your wings.
I cling to you; your right hand upholds me.

PSALM 63:7-8

NOT EVERY MOMMA'S STORY STARTS THE SAME WAY. The differences are vast and beautiful, but there was a universal moment that you, like every momma, experienced, which signaled the beginning. There was a special spark from heaven when you heard your baby's first cry. It was as if electricity coursed through your heart and somehow caused it to beat in the rhythm of motherhood. No matter how your baby arrived in your arms, that sound signaled the start of a completely new chapter in your life. Across the generations, this moment marks the beginning of a journey that is both thrilling and overwhelming.

When I brought my older daughter home from the hospital after she had spent a few days in the NICU, I laid her in her little crib in our tiny second-floor apartment. This was it; I was a momma on my own without nurses, doctors, or even my husband, who was preparing to go back to work. To say that I felt overwhelmed was an understatement!

Sometimes we feel like this, don't we, Momma? It's all brand-new, and it's up to us. The first time my daughter cried that day, my heart raced, and both of my legs cramped so badly that I could barely walk the short hallway to her room. But I held on to the walls and hobbled toward the sound of her cries. That's how being a momma of a newborn sometimes feels—like we are hanging on to whatever stability we can find and stumbling forward the best we can. Although we don't share the same experience, the same emotions accompany many mommas in those early days.

When he felt alone after fleeing to the wilderness, David sang to the Lord: "Because you are my help, I sing in the shadow of your wings. I cling to you; your right hand upholds me." When we grasp for something to hang on to, we can trust that God is our help. We can cling to Him and remember that His arms are big enough to hold us and our babies.

Tonight we pray for the momma *of a newborn. Lord, You know everything this momma is feeling. You know all her joys and all her fears. You know all the questions in her heart, and You have the answers. Tonight we ask that You help her feel Your presence surrounding her and her baby. Multiply her rest tonight and give her strength for the days ahead. Help her know she's doing a great job, and You are proud of her.*

We ask in Jesus's name, amen.

Creator God, thank You for this precious life. As much as I've anticipated bringing my baby home, I'm tired, and there is so much I don't know about this child and being a mom. Tonight I ask You to help me . . .

who is making the best decisions she can

If it is from God, you will not be able to stop these men;
you will only find yourselves fighting against God.

ACTS 5:39

THE HOLY SPIRIT HAD DESCENDED on Jesus's apostles (also called disciples) on the Day of Pentecost. The Holy Spirit had filled them with power from on high just as the Lord had promised. The apostles now went about sharing the gospel of Jesus, healing the sick, and setting free those possessed by demons.

As the religious leaders saw the crowds following the disciples, they became jealous and had the apostles arrested, much like they had done to Jesus just a few months before. But while these men were in jail, an angel came at night to set them free. He told them to go and continue preaching the gospel. By daybreak, the men were back in the Temple.

When the religious leaders sent for Peter and the apostles so they could be brought in for questioning, they were stunned to hear that the men were no longer in jail. When the leaders learned that the disciples were preaching in the Temple, they were so angry that they wanted them put to death. But Gamaliel, a respected leader and teacher, had this to say: "In the present case I advise you: Leave these men alone! Let them go! For if their purpose or activity is of human origin, it will fail. But if it is from God, you will not be able to stop these men; you will only find yourselves fighting against God" (Acts 5:38-39). You see, his opinion was very different from the rest of the leaders.

Momma, there are so many competing voices in your life. People offer advice on a million topics from breastfeeding to homeschooling to when to allow Internet access or give kids their own smartphones. Everyone has an opinion. If you don't hear it from someone in person, you will certainly hear about it on social media.

The key is to be like Gamaliel, because in the end this wise leader trusted the Lord to show what was true. And you are a wise momma who is the most experienced person when it comes to your own family. You can trust the Lord with your decisions. He will show you what is best for your children.

Tonight we pray for the momma *who is making the best decisions she can. Lord, there are so many competing voices saying what is right. She is a good momma, and she feels like she knows what is best for her kids. The weight of all the options is heavy, and the last thing she needs is to carry the burden of others' opinions on her decisions. Tonight we pray for peace for her uncertain mind. Bless her and give her wisdom.*

We ask in Jesus's name, amen.

Lord, please give me Your guidance and
peace as I work to make a good decision about . . .

whose mind never gets a break

*Do not conform to the pattern of this world, but be transformed by
the renewing of your mind. Then you will be able to test and
approve what God's will is—his good, pleasing and perfect will.*

ROMANS 12:2

IN THE FIRST FEW YEARS OF OUR MARRIAGE, Jared and I attended
only a handful of weddings. We married so young—at just nineteen
and twenty-three—that most of our friends didn't tie the knot
until many years later. But I loved weddings. I loved the planning,
the emotion, and the chance to serve in any way I could. It was
during a backyard ceremony that I gained a love not just of weddings but of wedding photography. A couple from our church was
holding a simple ceremony to renew their vows and needed an inex-
pensive photographer. I had a digital point-and-shoot camera that
I had used only to take photos of my new husband and our dog.

I had never photographed a wedding or any other event. But they weren't looking for extraordinary photos. They were just looking for someone who could document their day.

That small backyard wedding began a new season of life for me. I purchased a "photographer's camera" and created a website. I took online lessons from free Internet sources, and I offered my amateur services to anyone who would let me try.

I think my husband and I photographed over twenty weddings in those first few years, and our talents grew. We went to gorgeous locations. We were a part of so many special occasions. And I stay in touch with many of the brides I photographed more than ten years ago.

I have to be honest: When that season of life ended shortly after I became a momma, I was relieved. You might think wedding photographers would get breaks now and then, but from the time the wedding party arrives until the bride and groom make their celebrated getaway, there is no time to pause. Every moment is special. The entire day deserves documentation.

If I were to stop paying attention, something could go uncaptured, and there weren't any do-overs. From the dress and flowers to the family portraits, from the ceremony to the reception—every moment mattered. Every second was scheduled, and when there was no official wedding planner, as photographer I kept everything moving forward on schedule. My mind never got a break.

As mommas, everything feels special to us as well. We don't

want to let anyone down or miss any magical moments. We know that each day is unique, and we feel the weight of what could happen if we fail to capture the moment.

I know you keep mental lists of everything. I know you're tired, not just from what you're doing, but from what you're thinking and planning. You're tired of being the one to make sure everything moves forward because you're the coordinator of it all.

I often think about Paul on his missionary journeys to tell the world the Good News about Jesus. Paul was faithful to go exactly where the Holy Spirit directed exactly when the Holy Spirit told him to go there. Why? Because he knew that God had a perfect plan that was far better than anything he could come up with on his own.

Paul also had advice on how we can discern the Spirit's direction for our lives: "Do not conform to the pattern of this world, but be transformed by the renewing of your mind. Then you will be able to test and approve what God's will is—his good, pleasing and perfect will." God has so much insight to offer us. He has so much peace to add to our planning. If your mind needs a break, trust this: God won't forget one detail of whatever needs to be done. He's there with you through every magical moment and ordinary day.

Tonight we pray for the momma *whose mind never gets a break. Lord, from the time her eyes open until she falls asleep—and even when she wakes up in the middle of the night—she is thinking about what she needs to do next. She makes the hard decisions and the easy ones. She decides when to let things go or take things on. Her mind never stops. Tonight, Lord, we thank You for the rest You bring to her body, mind, emotions, and spirit. Help her give You all her cares tonight so her heart can settle.*

We ask in Jesus's name, amen.

God, please give me wisdom, direction, and peace
when it comes to all these people and tasks on my mind:

who wishes she weren't so anxious

Who of you by worrying can add a single hour to your life?

LUKE 12:25

WHEN I WAS GROWING UP IN THE NINETIES, there were all kinds of mommas in my neighborhood. Some moms worked while others stayed home. Some made peanut butter and jelly for lunch while others made mac and cheese. Running from backyard to backyard, I observed many different styles of motherhood. And long before I ever had kids, I knew the kind of momma I hoped to be. I wanted to be silly and spontaneous while also being a steady and safe place for my kids to share anything. I wanted to be the mom who said yes as often as she could while still maintaining healthy boundaries. I wanted to be the "let's go look at Christmas lights at 9:30 p.m.

on a school night" mom while also being the "we will not be late to school the next day or skip church on Sunday because we had fun too late the night before" mom.

Never on my list of aims or ambitions did I add the word *anxious*. Never once did I plan to be the momma who worries excessively or feels overwhelmed in ordinary circumstances. I didn't aspire to be the momma who checked, double-checked, and checked one more time just to make sure everything was okay. I didn't want to be the mom who said no just because she feared what might happen if she said yes.

Anxiety was never supposed to be a part of my story. My momma didn't plan for it to be a part of her story either. Nor did her momma before her. If you deal with overwhelming worry, I'm sure you never planned for it to be a part of yours. And if you're anything like me, you sometimes go through your days wondering why you're so anxious and wishing you weren't. You see other mommas who don't seem nearly as impacted by routine, day-to-day concerns. They seem to be able to "let go and let God" far more often than you could ever imagine doing. And you just wish that were your story as well.

I need to offer some hope for all of us today. God knew the exact mommas we would be when He placed children into our care. He chose us, knowing that during this season of life we would turn to Him and rely on Him to be our constant peace. Because the truth is, we cannot add one moment to our lives by worrying. Jesus made this clear: "Who of you by worrying can add a single hour to your life?" The understood answer is . . . none of us.

Worrying doesn't keep us safe. It doesn't add to our tranquility. No, my friend. But Jesus offers peace as a gift, and it is only through our proximity to Him that we are able to take what is in His hand. We cannot add to our lives by wishing or worrying, but we can greatly add to our lives by pausing and praying. Tonight let's do just that. Let's remember that while we might not have planned for this moment, this attitude, or this worry to be a part of our stories, God has written a far better chapter ahead for us. It's the one titled "Peace," and it's marked by His constant presence.

Tonight we pray for the momma *who wishes she weren't so anxious. Lord, she trusts You, she prays, she does her best to just stop being afraid. But no matter how hard she tries, her heart and mind race on. Tonight we ask You to do what only You can. May Your peace cover her like a blanket. Touch her mind and still her thoughts. You are with her and her family, and she trusts You. Help her rest tonight.*

We ask in Jesus's name, amen.

Lord, help me not feel so anxious about . . .

_____

_____

_____

who hopes she
is making the right choices

Don't urge me to leave you or to turn back from you.
Where you go I will go, and where you stay I will stay.
Your people will be my people and your God my God.

RUTH 1:16

THE DRIVE TO CALIFORNIA WITH everything we owned was longer than I had anticipated. As mile after mile passed, I hoped we had heard God clearly. I kept hoping we had made the right choice to move.

In Scripture we read about another woman, Ruth, who made the bold decision to leave her home behind. Do you know her story? Ruth grew up in Moab. During a famine in Israel, an Israelite couple, Elimelek and Naomi, emigrated to her country with their two sons. Ruth married one son, and another Moabite woman, Orpah, married the other. Sadly, Elimelek and both of his sons passed away, and the three women had to decide what to do next.

Upon hearing that the famine in Israel had ended, Naomi decided to return home. She released each of her daughters-in-law to return to her mother's house to marry a different man. Orpah decided to return to her people, but Ruth insisted on staying with Naomi: "Don't urge me to leave you or to turn back from you. Where you go I will go, and where you stay I will stay. Your people will be my people and your God my God."

I often wonder if Ruth ever questioned her decision to leave the land she had known her whole life to go on this journey to Judea with her mother-in-law. There was no guarantee that Ruth would find another husband to help them both live. They had no real plan. But God did.

The women were following the Lord's leading, traveling mile after mile. What neither knew was that they were walking toward the greatest adventure in God's plan. Ruth would marry a man named Boaz and would give birth to a son. This son's descendant would be our very Savior, Jesus the Messiah.

I picture this young woman of foreign descent walking many miles on a dusty road in the Middle East because of her decision to follow her mother-in-law and let her mother-in-law's God be her God. As a result, Ruth became one of the few women listed in the lineage of our Lord.

Momma, sometimes you can't see the impact or importance of

the decisions you make. But sometimes those decisions count for eternity, not just for you and for your family. After all, Ruth's decision was tied to salvation for the world. You may not always be sure you've made the right decision, but the Lord is with you and guiding you toward your destiny.

Tonight we pray for the momma *who hopes she is making the right choices. Lord, there are so many different roads to take and decisions to make. Rarely does she feel 100 percent confident when she chooses. Tonight she needs You to reassure her that she's on the right path and that You're the One guiding her. She hasn't missed it. She hasn't taken a wrong turn. She hasn't made it here by accident. She might have felt uncertain when she moved in this direction, but You haven't wavered. You are the voice she has been following, and it's all going to turn out okay. Give her peace tonight.*

We ask in Jesus's name, amen.

Lord, please continue guiding me on my journey to . . .

who needs to know that you care about every aspect of her life

You have searched me, LORD, and you know me. You know when I sit and when I rise; you perceive my thoughts from afar. You discern my going out and my lying down; you are familiar with all my ways.

PSALM 139:1-3

I WAS HOME FOR CHRISTMAS BREAK IN 1976 and had been invited by my church to speak at a regional women's conference. I was confident in who God was to me, and I wanted these women to know that despite my young age, my words were worthy of their attention. In addition to carefully crafting my message, I wanted to choose the right outfit to capture their interest and respect.

As I began considering what I would wear to such an event, I knew that I wanted to appear outwardly as confident as I felt within myself. Long maxi skirts were all the rage, and as I went through my suitcase, I was so glad that a good friend back at school had given me a skirt she no longer wore.

My friend might not have realized it, but God knew when and why I'd need her gift. It was something that could easily have been overlooked, but it didn't go unnoticed by me. God cared about even this simple aspect of my life.

Sometimes when we pray, we ask the Lord only about the big things—needs and dilemmas related to our family, our jobs, our church, and our community. But I wonder how often we pray about the smaller things that are also weighing on our hearts. We limit the God of the universe because we think He has to manage too many other important things to care about our "smaller needs." Do you know what I mean?

We might think to ourselves, *Well, that's something I can take care of, so why would I pray about it?* Perhaps we don't even think to seek God's help or wisdom for these lesser concerns because we assume the Lord has only so much time or interest.

But we know from Scripture that this is not true:

You have searched me, LORD, and you know me. You know when I sit and when I rise; you perceive my thoughts from afar. You discern my going out and my lying down; you are familiar with all my ways. Before a word is on my tongue you, LORD, know it completely. You hem me in behind and before, and you lay your hand upon me.

PSALM 139:1-5

I love the image of God hemming us in both behind and before. We are always shielded by His love, and His care and concern are all around us. He is omnipresent. That means that He is every-where. He isn't confined to one place in time as we are. He is our constant companion. He sees it all because He is with us through it all. Including Him in each moment of our day is as simple as whis-pering in our hearts our prayers about whatever is happening in that moment.

We can just turn our hearts toward His and ask for whatever we need, remembering that He always desires to meet us, lead us, and give us His peace.

Tonight we pray for the momma *who needs to know that You care about every aspect of her life. Lord, You know about every part of her. There is nothing that she must face alone. You care about her peace, her healing, and her hope. Tonight we ask that You'd help her find the right resources to bring her mind, body, and spirit to a place of wholeness. Heal every sad, anxious, overwhelmed, and hurting place within her. We are thankful that You are the God who heals. Help her realize Your presence in this moment.*

We ask in Jesus's name, amen.

Lord, I often pray about my big concerns,
but tonight I bring these situations to You as well:

who just needs a minute

When Jesus heard what had happened,
he withdrew by boat privately to a solitary place.

MATTHEW 14:13

AFTER THE MOVING TRUCK LEFT, I (Susan) stood in the empty bedroom closet and thought about all the things that had been stored there over the years. Of course, it's where I kept my clothes, but it's also where I stashed family pictures and artwork that I didn't want to store in the garage.

That closet didn't just hold items; it held moments. I'd often retreat to that quiet place where the clothes muffled any sound. It became a sanctuary and a refuge where even my thoughts quieted down. When something overwhelming happened and I needed to have a private phone conversation with one of my sisters, my mom, or my best friend, this was my retreat. When I just needed to pour out my heart to God, I would sit on the floor between the coats and have what I called "just a moment."

On this particular day, I knew I was standing in this closet for the last time to think about the memories it held. The Lord was leading us to our next space.

Perhaps you have your own quiet place for when you need to be alone. There were moments when even Jesus needed to withdraw. Scripture tells us about one particularly poignant time after His cousin, John the Baptist, was killed. John had been a strong voice, calling people to repentance and calling out the sin that separated them from God. No one's sin was off-limits; John publicly rebuked even those in high governmental positions. Because of this, he was thrown in prison and ultimately put to death.

John was the same cousin who had leapt in his mother's womb when Jesus's mother, Mary, came to visit Elizabeth. This is the cousin who had baptized Jesus in the River Jordan and heard the voice from heaven declaring, "This is my Son, whom I love; with him I am well pleased" (Matthew 3:17). We might assume they had seen each other regularly throughout their childhoods at family events and at the Temple on feast days. John was important to Jesus's life and ministry. So when Jesus heard the news of John's death, "he withdrew by boat privately to a solitary place."

Momma, it is okay to take a moment for yourself when you need one, but especially when you receive news that is particularly hard to bear. It's okay to take a moment for yourself to shed tears that will only be seen by your heavenly Father. It's okay to take a moment to remember that God understands your grief. You have a Savior who is sympathetic to your sufferings.

Friend, life can often be overwhelming, and just because you are a momma does not mean you have to process everything for all the world to see. It's okay to step back when you can and find a place just for yourself and Jesus.

Tonight we pray for the momma *who needs a minute. Lord, she might need a minute to think, to breathe, or to be alone. She might need a minute to process the news or sadness or her own racing thoughts. She might need a minute when she isn't the one in charge of making decisions. Lord, You see this momma and all she needs. Help her find the moment her heart craves, and meet her in it. Give her space to laugh, cry, vent, or breathe deeply with You. Thank You for caring about this momma's heart and mind. Wrap her in Your peace.*

We ask in Jesus's name, amen.

Jesus, I ask for Your peace about . . .

_____

_____

_____

who is doing a good job

I will ask the Father, and he will give you another
advocate to help you and be with you forever.

JOHN 14:16

EVERYBODY LOVES A GOOD MOVIE about the athlete who was told that they couldn't accomplish something . . . but who defies all odds to rise up and overcome. As we watch them struggle, we realize that most of the battle takes place in their mind. What will they listen to—the voices of defeat or victory? Will they overcome their own fears and triumph in the end? Will they catch the ball for the winning touchdown? Will they run the race in record time? The final scenes of the movie are typically full of last-minute victories, cheering crowds, and golden trophies or medals.

Being a momma is kind of like being in one of those

movies . . . except without the awards, cheering crowds, or Hall of Fame. Every morning we rise and have to overcome our internal dialogue that tells us we are not good enough or strong enough to be good moms. Our past defeats rush to the front of our minds, which makes it hard to keep going forward. We remember every time we struck out or dropped the ball. We think of all the moments we just barely missed making a key play. We are so very hard on ourselves.

Here is the good news about the momma race: Our Lord promised us that we would never be alone. Jesus told us that after He ascended to His Father, He would send to us another Comforter who would also be our Advocate "to help you and be with you forever." The Holy Spirit is our everything coach! He teaches us what we need to know, and He comforts us with the words of the Father. He reminds us to forget what is behind and to "press on toward the goal to win the prize for which God has called [us] heavenward in Christ Jesus" (Philippians 3:14).

Momma, you may not receive the applause of a cheering crowd in a big stadium. You may feel unnoticed or overlooked. But every decision you make, every meal you prepare, every time you tuck your children in at night is a win for your family. It all counts in this life. It all has eternal impact as you raise children who look to Jesus in their own lives. Tonight, Momma, we see you and we are cheering for you.

Tonight we pray for the momma *who is doing a good job. Lord, she does so much for her family. Each day she makes decisions and sacrifices. She puts her family before herself again and again. She tries so hard. She does such a good job, but she isn't told nearly as often as she deserves. So, Lord, please lean in and whisper to her heart. Help her hear You saying, "I see it all, and I am so proud of you." Help her hear it . . . and believe it. She's a good mom. Silence every fear and lie that would tell her otherwise.*

We ask in Jesus's name, amen.

Father, thank You for sending Your Spirit to be my Advocate. I ask Him to remind me . . .

who is grateful
for her own momma

*Jesus said to them, "Come and have breakfast." None of the disciples
dared ask him, "Who are you?" They knew it was the Lord. Jesus came,
took the bread and gave it to them, and did the same with the fish.*

JOHN 21:12-13

WHEN I WAS A LITTLE GIRL, my grandma thought that it was very
important to have starched curtains up in every room. Now my
own momma was busy raising young children and did not have the
time to starch her own curtains—so my grandma decided to help.
Every Saturday, I would walk over to her house. After feeding me a
lunch of freshly made meatballs, Grandma would hand me a dollar
to buy her some boiled ham at the deli. Just before I left her house,
she'd hand me a grocery bag holding freshly laundered and starched
kitchen and bedroom curtains that I took home to my mother.

I have thought about that grocery bag of curtains many times over the decades. It was like a sack of love that she sent home with me. It said all the things that the generations didn't really say out loud back then. It told my mom, *I see how busy you are.* It said, *I want you to know I am here for you.* It said, *I want you to have nice things,* and it said in the loudest of voices, *I love you.* I carried that love note home carefully. I didn't want to wrinkle a single panel. My momma let me help put them up when I got home. To this day, when I hang my own curtains, I think about how grateful my momma was for my grandma and her love notes, which looked like curtains in a brown grocery sack. There are so many ways to show love.

Scripture contains a wonderful story about how our Lord showed Peter that He still loved him by making him breakfast on the beach. Peter had a right to wonder. On the night Jesus was brought for trial, the religious leaders took Him first to the high priest's house. Peter followed and stood in the courtyard by the fire. A servant looked closely at him and said, "This man was with him" (Luke 22:56). But Peter denied knowing Jesus. Later another person said, "You also are one of them" (Luke 22:58). But Peter denied it again. Finally someone insisted that Peter, a Galilean, must have been with Jesus, and Peter denied Jesus for a third time, saying, "I don't know what you're talking about!" (Luke 22:60). In that moment, a rooster crowed, and Jesus looked straight at Peter, causing him to remember that the Lord had foretold he would deny knowing Jesus three times. Peter then left the courtyard and cried bitter tears.

But that wasn't the end of the story. After our Lord's resurrection, Peter, a fisherman by trade, decided to go fishing. He and his partners caught nothing until a familiar voice called to them from the beach: "Throw your net on the right side of the boat and you will find some" (John 21:6). When the net was instantly filled with fish, John said, "It is the Lord!" (John 21:7).

> When they landed, they saw a fire of burning coals there with fish on it, and some bread. Jesus said to them, "Bring some of the fish you have just caught." So Simon Peter climbed back into the boat and dragged the net ashore. It was full of large fish, 153, but even with so many the net was not torn. Jesus said to them, "Come and have breakfast."
>
> JOHN 21:9-12

While they were bringing in their catch, the Lord was preparing breakfast for them. This was such an act of love. It said, *I came to the place that you love, the sea where you catch fish.* It said, *I prepared a table for you to nourish yourselves.* He knew that the road had been hard. It said, *I see you and who you are.* And it said, *You're still welcome to come and eat with me, Peter.*

Likewise, our own mommas sometimes reflect the love of Christ to us in their simple acts of kindness, empathy, and compassion. At times, other caring women in our lives teach us about the nature of God by loving us. For that we are so very thankful. Whether you have a momma by birth or by choice, each momma in our lives is a gift. Let's pause and thank the Lord for them now.

Tonight we pray for the momma *who is grateful for her own momma. Lord, she is thinking about the unconditional love her momma gives and the helping hands she offers when needed. Her momma's smile encourages her when she feels down. When she is crying, her momma's tears join in her own. Lord, we ask that You bless each of our mommas tonight. Grant them a good night of sleep and strength for tomorrow.*

We ask in Jesus's name, amen.

Lord, thank you for my own momma and the other women who support me on my parenting journey:

_____

_____

_____

_____

who is exhausted to her core

*Suddenly an angel touched him, and
said to him, "Arise and eat."*

1 KINGS 19:5, NKJV

SHORTLY AFTER JARED AND I MOVED our family to California,
all three of our kids tested positive for the flu. They seemed to get
super sick all at once, so while Jared was at work one evening, I took
the kids to a walk-in clinic on my own. It just couldn't wait until
morning, and we didn't have a primary care doctor established yet.

Doctor visits with one child can be stressful, but with three
young kids all running high fevers (and their emotions running
high as well), the hour we spent at the clinic felt like an eternity.
But the exhaustion had just begun.

It took the pharmacy an hour to fill the prescriptions after they sent me a notification saying they were ready. There was no one to call for help with the kids. That evening it was just me . . . and the Lord. I was exhausted to my core.

Elijah, a prophet of God, wasn't a stranger to the stress that comes from having to stand alone to do what God has called you to do. The Lord had sent Elijah to confront His people, who had fallen into idol worship. The ruler of the day, Ahab, was being influenced by a wicked woman, Jezebel, and God's people were confused and living in complete disobedience to Him. So led by the Lord, Elijah called the people of God together and put the idol gods to a test. He said to the people, "You call on the name of your gods, and I will call on the name of the Lord; and the God who answers by fire, He is God" (1 Kings 18:24, NKJV).

When the one true God came down in fire and consumed Elijah's sacrifice, the people of God declared, "The Lord, He is God!" Elijah said to them, "Seize the prophets of Baal! Do not let one of them escape" (1 Kings 18:39-40, NKJV). Jezebel, hearing that her prophets had been destroyed, threatened Elijah's life. And despite having seen God move mightily, Elijah ran.

The exact distance he traveled is unknown, but we can estimate that he ran over one hundred miles, left his servant in a certain town, and went another day's journey into the wilderness. And when he was done running, he lay down and told the Lord how he really felt. He was exhausted from all he had faced. He was exhausted from all he had done. He was exhausted by all the fear in his heart. He wasn't just tired; he was weary to his bones. Listen to what happened next:

> Suddenly an angel touched him, and said to him, "Arise and eat." . . . There by his head was a cake baked on coals, and a jar of water. So he ate and drank, and lay down again. And the angel of the LORD came back the second time, and touched him, and said, "Arise and eat, because the journey is too great for you." So he arose, and ate and drank; and he went in the strength of that food forty days and forty nights.
>
> I KINGS 19:5-8, NKJV

Do you know what I love about this story? No, it's not just that Elijah was tired and took a nap while an angel made him a snack. I love that God supernaturally provided both the rest and the food he needed to give him strength for the journey ahead. While it would be wonderful to have anyone cook me a nice meal, tuck me into bed, and say, "Rest up," I take so much comfort in knowing that God knows exactly what I need for the days that are coming. And as the angel told Elijah, "Eat, because the journey is too great for you," the Lord tells us, "I am your daily bread. Take and eat because I'm your strength."

My friend, He knows you're tired. He knows all you have faced. He knows you need a deep heart reset. Let's pray and ask Him to step in and touch the places in our hearts that only He can restore.

Tonight we pray for the momma *who is exhausted to her core. Lord, she's not just sleepy. She's not just tired. She is at the end of herself. She has given every last ounce of her strength. Maybe it was something unexpected that came up and added stress, or maybe it was just a little bit of everything this week. No matter the cause of her weariness, Lord, we are asking You to help her. We are asking You to supernaturally strengthen her mind, body, and spirit. Remove all anxiety, stress, worry, and exhaustion and replace them with peace, joy, and hope for tomorrow.*

We ask in Jesus's name, amen.

Heavenly Father, I ask for Your supernatural
strength and endurance as I . . .

who feels like
she can't catch up

Peace I leave with you; my peace I give you. I do not give to you as the
world gives. Do not let your hearts be troubled and do not be afraid.

JOHN 14:27

EVERY WEDNESDAY NIGHT, Mark and I watch the popular television show *Survivor*, in which contestants test their ability to
survive in a remote location with strangers. The winner of a weekly
challenge—physical, mental, or both—is given immunity from
being voted out that week. Contestants want to remain in the game
as long as they can because the last remaining participant wins one
million dollars.

One of the challenges on this show reminds me so much of
motherhood that I chuckle whenever I see it. The first rule is that
the contestants have to keep one hand behind their backs at all

times. Next, a ball is dropped into a contraption that looks like a small roller coaster. It goes down the chute and through a series of gates and turnstiles until it comes flying out at the bottom. The objective is to catch that ball before it hits the ground. Every few minutes another ball is added, and the timing is critical to prevent the first, second, or third ball from dropping before being caught. It takes concentration, physical dexterity, and the ability to time everything just right.

When I watch this show, I think to myself, *Put in the first ball, do the laundry; add the second ball, make the meals; add the third ball, provide transportation to sports practice; add the fourth ball . . .* I think you get it. Some days all you can think about is how not to drop anything or anyone and just keep up because life never slows down and the balls never stop flying through the chutes. But inevitably something comes flying at us, and we don't have our timing just right. Something important gets dropped, and we feel like we will never catch up.

All the responsibilities that come together seem to be taunting, *You'll never catch me! You can't handle this! You are too far behind!* But those are lies from the enemy of our hearts that you don't have to listen to. Our Lord promised us: "Peace I leave with you; my peace I give you. I do not give to you as the world gives. Do not let your hearts be troubled and do not be afraid."

Jesus can and will replace those noisy thoughts with His peace. He will help us keep moving forward in His love. He keeps the whole world spinning, and yet He carefully holds our hearts too. We don't have to be afraid of what is right in front of us and what is coming our way because the Lord has promised us His peace. Let's thank Him for that peace right now as we pray together.

Tonight we pray for the momma *who feels like she can't catch up. Lord, it might be her children, the housework, the bills, or her relationships. She might feel like she'll never measure up to her friends who seem to have it all together. She might feel a little bit behind in so many areas. And just when she makes progress in one area, she feels as if she falls behind in another. Lord, bring peace and rest to this momma's racing heart. Silence all the swirling lies that tell her she'll never make it. Help her take ground in the areas that seem beyond her reach.*

We ask in Jesus's name, amen.

Lord, give me energy, creativity, and a fresh perspective in these areas where I feel so far behind:

_____

_____

_____

_____

whose faith feels tested

God did say, "You must not eat fruit from the tree that is in the middle of the garden, and you must not touch it, or you will die."

GENESIS 3:3

OH, EVE, WHY DID YOU EAT THE FRUIT? We have thought this countless times over the years. Haven't you? Everything changed in the moment she took that fateful bite. It permanently changed life for all of us—the entire human race. *Why?*

Everyone has asked this question at some point in their lives: "Why, God?" "Why did this happen to me or my loved one?" "Why do bad things happen to good people?" "Why do children get sick and pass away?" "Why is there war and famine?" It's the eternal question that seems to have an elusive answer. Have you ever asked God why?

We find the answer to this age-old question in Genesis 3. The moment Eve disobeyed God's only command—not to eat the fruit of the tree of the knowledge of good and evil in the Garden—sin entered the world and humans began to die. The perfect relationship, the perfect world, and the perfect creation ended.

People now lived by the sweat of their brow and the toil of their hands. The ground fought against them, producing thorns and weeds. Life was very different from when the first man and woman, Adam and Eve, walked with the Lord in the cool of the day.

That's the reason, my friend. That's the reason for suffering and sadness. That's the reason for heartache and hopelessness. The answer is that we live in a broken world. It fractured with the first taste of the forbidden fruit.

When people ask us why something bad has happened, we remind them that we are all broken, right down to our DNA. No aspect of life is untouched by that original sin in the Garden. But God has always had a plan so that we never have to face our brokenness alone.

Perhaps your faith is being tested. You have trusted God in faith, and you feel as if He owes you an answer. Tonight can I remind you that He is making a way for you to travel through this trying season? He isn't waiting to see how you fare on the other side, what your faith will be when you get through it, or if you choose the door of hope or hopelessness. He is carrying you.

Momma, whatever crisis of faith you may be going through right now, lean on your relationship with the Lord. Lean on what you know His heart to be for you and your family. You know why bad things happen. But Jesus, the One who wages war on all injustice, is Faithful and True. You can continue to trust Him.

Tonight we pray for the momma *whose faith feels tested in this season. Lord, she has hard questions. She wants to know why. She doesn't understand what You are doing, Lord, or where You have been. Tonight we ask You to comfort this momma as only You can. Speak the words her heart needs to find rest and trust again. Help her see exactly where You have been . . . right there with her all along. You can handle her questions. Give her supernatural faith so she can get to the other side of this time in her life.*

We ask in Jesus's name, amen.

Jesus, even when my faith feels tested,
I trust You in these specific areas:

who puts her children first

Jesus said, "Let the little children come to me, and do not hinder them,
for the kingdom of heaven belongs to such as these."

MATTHEW 19:14

DURING THE WINTER OLYMPICS a number of years ago, a commercial grabbed my attention. Inspirational music played softly over a series of short clips showing mommas picking up their little ones as they learned to walk, ice-skate, and ski. Then it captured these mommas getting their children to practice, finding what they needed for training, and lifting them up after they failed and fell again and again. We see the children and the mommas grow together. The commercial ends by showing the final results of all the hard effort: The athletes take the medal, win the race, or nail the jump. There at the end are the grown children turning to their moms, remembering who was with them through it all.

There's a reason so many award acceptance speeches include the words, "I want to thank my momma." Why? Because even though children might not find the occasion to say it out loud very often, they realize who was there beside them through everything. They remember the role their mommas played in all they achieved.

The Gospel of Matthew includes a story about people bringing their children for Jesus to bless. The disciples rebuked them, but Jesus corrected his disciples: "Let the little children come to me, and do not hinder them, for the kingdom of heaven belongs to such as these." Our Lord saw the children and counted them as valuable. He proclaimed them important and invited them to come to Him.

Like Jesus, when we look at our little children, we cherish them. We see them through His eyes. And we remember that while the work might not seem important, the Lord values it and them greatly.

Momma, when our children are little, we don't think that they see the love we show them by our daily sacrifices. But they are watching everything and coming to conclusions they don't even have the words for yet. As mommas, we carry our love for our children in our hearts and our minds and show it through our words and our actions. But as we do this, it is so important to remember that the Lord loves them, blesses them, and declares that His Kingdom belongs to "such as these." It's for Him that we continue to make them our priority.

Tonight we pray for the momma *who puts her children first.*

She sacrifices her sleep and her time, but some days she looks around at all she has to put down so she can carry the love she has for her children. It feels like so much. Lord, You know the power of this gift of love. Remind this momma that no part of her love has ever been wasted. You will use every bit of what she has given for the good of her children. Pour encouragement into her heart now. Bless her tonight.

We ask in Jesus's name, amen.

Lord, help me to love my children well again tomorrow. For now, I turn over to You my concerns for them:

who needs patience

The Holy Spirit produces this kind of fruit in our lives: love, joy, peace, patience, kindness, goodness, faithfulness, gentleness, and self-control.

GALATIANS 5:22-23, NLT

AS A MOMMA WITH TWO IN MIDDLE SCHOOL and one in elementary, I have this habit of rushing through life. I overschedule myself; I overestimate what I can accomplish, and as a result, I often find myself overwhelmed and overtired. I feel like I can rest only when everything is done. So I scurry through my days, constantly feeling behind, expecting my family to experience the same sense of continual urgency, and frustrated when those I love take "extra" from my already overextended schedule.

Don't they know I don't have time for trivial sibling fights? Doesn't my husband see that I don't have time for this last-minute event he has added to our family calendar? Doesn't the world get that I'm already spread thin and could snap at any second?

Listen, I fully understand that you might not relate to these sentiments in this season of your life. Perhaps you have strong boundaries around your time and take great care to protect your heart's emotional health. But can you pull from your memory a time when you found yourself lacking patience? Can you recall the desire to be the calm, centered, compassionate momma when what you felt instead was the confusion and chaos of a cluttered calendar and heart?

My friend, many seasons of life require us to offer patience to those we love and live alongside. There are situations in motherhood and outside the four walls of our home in which we must draw from the patient part of our hearts. But the apostle Paul reminds us of an important truth concerning this attribute: "The Holy Spirit produces this kind of fruit in our lives: love, joy, peace, patience, kindness, goodness, faithfulness, gentleness, and self-control."

Patience is a fruit of God's Spirit at work in our lives, and that means it is grown by pressing into our relationship with Him. Patience is a by-product of spending time listening to Jesus's heart and following His Spirit. When we allow Him to have access to those rushed places in our lives, when we invite Him to come close and rearrange our priorities, when we yield to His ways and not to the hurry of our own plans, He reminds us of what we likely knew all along: "Be patient" isn't something we can just add to our to-do list; it requires us to rely on Jesus and invite Him into even the most ordinary parts of our day.

Tonight we pray for the momma *who needs patience. Lord, it's all just too much right now. She is trying to be kind and loving and understanding, but she is finding herself needing a break or a breath or just a pause to regather herself. She knows her family needs peace. She knows there is stress in her home, and she wants to respond kindly and calmly. Help her have patience with herself and her family. Give her an extra measure of grace.*

We ask in Jesus's name, amen.

Holy Spirit, help me to reflect Your
patience toward me when it comes to . . .

who loves her sister (by birth or by choice)

Now Jesus loved Martha and her sister and Lazarus.

JOHN 11:5

TWO OF THE WOMEN WE SEE MOST in the Gospels are Martha and Mary, the sisters from Bethany. We've spoken about them a few times already, but now we want to focus on an important aspect of their relationship: They stuck together.

They were together when Jesus came to their home for a visit. They sought the Lord together when their brother was sick. They both approached Jesus when He came after their brother's death. Mary and Martha were a pair.

We love that we can see the many parts of these sisters' lives. We watch them rejoicing, struggling, and ugly crying. We can imagine the stress of hosting Jesus and His entire company. We can imagine the shared grief after their brother's death. And we can almost hear the two women yell for joy when Lazarus came back to life.

Through it all, they had each other. They were just like us, only they lived about two thousand years ago. From their relationship, we can see that being sisters is much the same across the ages. Being a woman whom another calls her sister is a gift.

Not all of us are born into families with a Mary for our Martha or a Martha for our Mary. Not all of us grow alongside women who know our stories or share our history. But the Gospels introduce us to other female followers of Jesus—women like Joanna, Mary Magdalene, and Mary, the mother of Jesus—who became like family to Mary and Martha. These women weren't sisters by blood, but they were sisters by choice. They shared a common story of following Jesus throughout His ministry and being a part of His family.

Tonight we want you to pause for a moment and think about the sisters of your story. Think about the women who have shared in your grief, celebrated in your joy, held you in your suffering, and carried you with their own strength. And then pause and think about the sister you have been to others.

Tonight we pray for the momma *who loves her sister, whether they're connected by birth or by choice. Father, they have been through happy times, sad times, and difficult times together, and they still love each other. May they hold one another up in prayer tonight. We ask for a special blessing on each one. Bless them and their families with peace, joy, and strength.*

We ask in Jesus's name, amen.

Lord, I thank You for _____,
my sister by birth or choice who gets me
and gives so much of herself to me.

who doesn't know
what to pray right now

Cast all your anxiety on him because he cares for you.

1 PETER 5:7

"I know that God must get tired of hearing from me, Becky," my friend told me with a small laugh. "There always seems to be something wrong that I have to pray about."

I smiled, offering her the gift of understanding but knowing that my friend's view of God's attitude toward her wasn't quite right.

God never grows tired of hearing from my friend, just like He never gets tired of hearing from any of His children. In what seemed to be a simple comment, my friend was expressing a much deeper concern. She felt as if her life had an ever-lengthening list of needs to address. There were people she loved who were sick, there was an impossible deadline to meet, and there were major life transitions that required her to make some serious changes. She was feeling the weight of issues inside her home as well as at work and among her friends and community.

"There's so much to tell Him about," she added. "I don't even know where to start!" Those words I understood completely. When we feel as if God needs to step in and do what only He can for everyone we know and everything we are a part of, the emotional weight of those burdens can be nearly unbearable. But Scripture offers this important instruction for how to handle those cares: "Do not be anxious about anything, but in every situation, by prayer and petition, with thanksgiving, present your requests to God" (Philippians 4:6).

God is a kind Father who wants us to come to Him with all our joys and concerns. He wants us to find rest for our exhausted and overwhelmed hearts in Him. Sure, He already knows everything we are facing, but He wants us to seek Him, knowing that when we do, we will find Him. We will find His guidance, His strength, His peace, and the promise that wherever His presence is, we will have everything we need.

If you're in a place where your prayer list is longer than your grocery list, your concerns far outweigh any celebrations, and your heart feels so sick with worry, know this: God is listening. He has heard your prayers. He has heard the words you haven't even whispered out loud yet. And He never ever grows tired of talking with you.

Tonight we pray for the momma *who doesn't even know what to pray right now. Lord, if she could, she would write You a letter that is one hundred pages long, detailing every joy, sorrow, heartache, and burden that has filled her heart. Lord, You know them all. Please surround this momma with everything and everyone she needs tonight. Please grant her sweet, restorative rest.*

We ask in Jesus's name, amen.

Father, when I don't even know what to pray,
thank You for understanding what's on my heart about . . .

_____

_____

_____

_____

_____

_____

_____

_____

_____

_____

who is ready for change

"For I know the plans I have for you,"
declares the Lord, *"plans to prosper you and not to harm you,*
plans to give you hope and a future."

JEREMIAH 29:11

For forty years, I wore my hair in a simple bob. Deciding it might finally be time for a change, I told a stylist who had just returned from a big hairstyling conference to "do something different." I gave her complete freedom to do whatever was new and exciting, sure that I would love it. Once she laid down her shears and spun me toward the mirror, I put my glasses back on, eager to see what she had done.

Fresh from the conference, this hairstylist had taken my words to heart and with great freedom had given me the most outlandish haircut I have ever had in my entire life. I had pointy hair in every direction in a very strange shade of purplish red.

I hadn't quite processed how different it looked until I went to the elementary school to pick up my daughter. When she and the other students saw me, my daughter's little friend started crying and said, "Change it back!" with big sobs. I think my new look actually scared her!

I have thought about this many times over the years. There is an old saying that change is the one thing you can count on. It is not always something we look forward to, however. Sometimes it can be quite upsetting, particularly when we discover that something we thought was in our power is actually beyond our control. Change can be fun and exciting. But change can also be scary.

Momma, if you're waiting for the Lord to step in and do something new, take heart in remembering that He is never surprised. While change might be unplanned, we have the Lord working out the details.

The prophet Jeremiah reassured the Jewish exiles in Babylon with these words from God: "'I know the plans I have for you,' declares the LORD, 'plans to prosper you and not to harm you, plans to give you hope and a future.'" His heart toward us is just as loving and good. Tonight let's give God permission to do whatever He thinks is best and trust that whatever the outcome, He has a hope and future for us that is good.

Tonight we pray for the momma *who is ready for change. Lord, she is caught in an endless cycle and just needs to know it won't always be this way. She is seeking help or hope or fresh happiness. She needs to see that it won't always be as hard or exhausting as it is right now. Lord, send Your Spirit to bring fresh winds of change. Help her believe as she goes to sleep tonight that tomorrow everything could be different in the best possible way. Address every anxiety and give this momma hope tonight. Fill her heart with peace.*

We ask in Jesus's name, amen.

Father, send Your Spirit to help me with change in this area:

_____

_____

_____

_____

_____

_____

_____

_____

_____

who is grateful for friends

A friend loves at all times.

PROVERBS 17:17

MY SWEET HUSBAND, MARK, has a friend he has known since elementary school. They don't see each other often these days because they live in different states, but he listens to this friend's advice and respects him. We have had many discussions about their conversations on important topics. I learn a lot from these exchanges, though I always laugh when I think of how my husband starts these stories with me: "My friend Tim says . . ." I stop and think, *You could just say Tim.* But Mark uses his full title: "My friend Tim." I thought this was so strange until I realized that I do it too!

I keep in touch with a few friends from elementary school, high school, and college. When I am telling someone about a conversation I've had with one of them, I always start by saying "My friend Rosemary" or "My friend Ellen."

It's not as if my husband and I know seven Tims, Rosemarys, or Ellens. I'm not sure we know even two. But we have attached being a friend to their name. Do you do that? It is such an honor to be called someone's friend, especially when that relationship has extended over many years!

Proverbs 17:17 tells us, "A friend loves at all times." Proverbs 18:24 says, "There is a friend who sticks closer than a brother." At times in my own life, it was easier to talk to a friend than my own family. There is something about that one step of separation that can bring perspective to a problem. Sometimes you just need your friend to listen with compassion.

If you don't have lots of close friends, let me remind you tonight that the Lord is our friend, and He stays closer than a brother! He certainly is the One who loves us at all times!

Tonight let's think about our earthly friends who have been with us through thick and thin. Let's pray and be grateful for them and to the Lord for bringing them into our lives. Next time you introduce someone close to you, consider saying these words: "This is my friend . . . ," and be blessed knowing they are in your life!

Tonight we pray for the momma *who is grateful for friends. Lord, she leans hard on these women who walk beside her, and they lean on her when needed. They help each other and hold each other up. In good times they laugh and in hard times they cry together. Lord, we are so grateful for the friends that You've brought into our lives. Please bless each one.*

We pray in Jesus's name, amen.

Jesus, I want to say a special thank You for my friend
_____, who has loved me so well. Most of all,
I'm grateful that You are the friend who will never fail me!

_____

_____

_____

_____

_____

_____

_____

_____

who wants to get it right

God is faithful, who has called you into fellowship with his Son,
Jesus Christ our Lord.

1 CORINTHIANS 1:9

THE WALLS SHOOK, AND A LARGE BOOM echoed through the hall-way. I was in the school's main office as a volunteer preparing for the upcoming spring festival. I stepped out of the office and walked to the front doors of the school. Surely, a bus had lost control and some-how hit the building. But there was no bus—only a plume of smoke rising from the downtown skyline. The air was filled with the sounds of sirens. So many sirens. I couldn't figure out what was happening.

I tried to call my husband, who worked downtown, but he didn't answer. His office phone didn't pick up either. Then the phones in the school office started to ring. It was April 19, 1995, and none of us knew yet what we were about to face together. A bombing had taken place in downtown Oklahoma City, and our country, state, and personal lives would never be the same.

So many decisions needed to be made immediately for our family. Were we safe where we were? Was my husband safe so close to the bombing? Did I need to get to him? I was trying to make decisions with no experience to lean on and very little information available.

Soon I was able to reach Mark by phone. His building, just a few blocks from the blast site, had sustained minor damage. He was okay, but our lives were still directly touched by this disaster. The church we attended was across the street from the demolished building, and we could no longer meet there.

Moving forward, there was the shared trauma of our community members and neighbors, but we were all just trying to make the best decisions for our own families. We wanted to get our responses to this event right. I knew how I responded would mark my daughters' lives forever. It was a challenge I hadn't been expecting.

Momma, the events you're navigating are different from my own, but I hope you see that in every decision we make, we share a common goal: We want what is best for our children. The truth is, so does the Lord. Replaying the moments of your life from the past and wondering if you did it right with the information you had doesn't change what unfolded in that moment. It may have seemed as if no one told you what to do and no one told you what was going to happen next. You felt unprepared or perhaps currently feel unprepared for what you're facing now. But here's what I want you to see: The Lord was the One who led you. He showed you what to do. He helped you make hard decisions in the past, and He will help you make every hard decision in the future. He is trustworthy. As Paul says, "God is faithful, who has called you into fellowship with his Son, Jesus Christ our Lord." We might not get every moment right, but the first right step in every new journey is the one directed by the Lord.

Tonight we pray for the momma *who wants to get it right. Lord, she doesn't want to make any mistakes because her children are so important to her. Lord, she is putting so much pressure on herself that she's lost her peace and her joy. Now tonight we ask that You would remind this momma that loving her children is enough in this moment. She doesn't have to be perfect because only You are. Please help her to rest tonight and wake up tomorrow with renewed peace and hope.*

We ask in Jesus's name, amen.

Lord, please help me get this right:

_____

_____

_____

_____

who needs to know today mattered

His master replied,
"Well done, good and faithful servant!"

MATTHEW 25:21

MOMMA, YOU MAY FEEL EXHAUSTED MOST DAYS. We do too. But, like us, you trust the Lord with all your heart. You understand the gift your children are to your life even when they require so much of your time and effort. In Scripture, we read that Jesus had much to say about those who cared for His precious treasures.

Jesus used stories to teach. Men and women would hear His words and apply the lessons of the stories to their lives. One story Jesus tells is known as the Parable of the Three Servants. It speaks about the Kingdom of Heaven and the work that must be done, but I believe that if we listen closely to Jesus's words, we'll see that He's speaking directly to us.

Jesus said a man was going on a long journey: "He called together his servants and entrusted his money to them while he was gone. He gave five bags of silver to one, two bags of silver to another, and one bag of silver to the last—dividing it in proportion to their abilities. He then left on his trip" (Matthew 25:14-15, NLT).

While the man was away on his journey, each of the three men entrusted with his finances invested the money differently.

The servant who received the five bags of silver began to invest the money and earned five more. The servant with two bags of silver also went to work and earned two more. But the servant who received the one bag of silver dug a hole in the ground and hid the master's money.

After a long time their master returned from his trip and called them to give an account of how they had used his money. The servant to whom he had entrusted the five bags of silver came forward with five more and said, "Master, you gave me five bags of silver to invest, and I have earned five more."

The master was full of praise. "Well done, my good and faithful servant. You have been faithful in handling this small amount, so now I will give you many more responsibilities. Let's celebrate together!"

MATTHEW 25:16-21, NLT

The Lord likewise praised the one who invested the two bags of silver given to him by his master. But the Lord did not have any praise for the one who buried his gift in fear. Only those who understood what they had been entrusted with received the praise.

Momma, can you hear the voice of the Father today praising all of your efforts? What you did today mattered. You are doing a good job. Has anyone told you that in a while? As a momma in her fortieth year of motherhood, let me offer some words of encouragement to you right now. Listen closely. You are a good momma. How do I know? Because the hallmark of a good momma is one who cares deeply about her children, the one who loves the Lord, the one who tries her best even if she isn't perfect. Good moms know that even when they are exhausted and ready for the day to be over, their children have been entrusted to them by their Father in heaven. So they turn their hearts toward Him and remember that they don't just love their children well for the sake of their kids—they love their children well because they are gifts from God.

Your heavenly Father is proud of you. And just as He said to the faithful servant, He says to you now, "Well done, my good and faithful servant.... Let's celebrate together!"

Tonight we pray for the momma *who needs to know today mattered. Lord, there are long days and then there are days like these when she just wants rest. She did well today, Lord. She might not feel like it, but she did. She did her best. She is a good momma. And she deserves to be told that. Lord, thank You for strengthening this momma. Multiply her rest tonight and fill her with peace.*

We ask in Jesus's name, amen.

Father, I'm so tired, but I want to love my
children well tomorrow. Please grant me
rejuvenating rest and a heart full of . . .

who is so hard on herself

Love . . . keeps no record of wrongs.

1 CORINTHIANS 13:4-5

I WAS SITTING IN MY OFFICE WORKING long after my three kids had fallen asleep. I would rather have been sleeping myself, but with my lengthy to-do list and the overscheduled week ahead, I was stealing minutes wherever I could find them.

To be honest, I felt as if I had been borrowing too many moments from my family and spending them on work. And I was still coming up short, unable to get it all done. I was staring at a computer screen at ten minutes to midnight, but my mind was anything but focused on what I had to do. I was remembering my day, my previous week, my last few years. It was as if my mind was replaying all the moments I had kept in a record of my wrongs.

That's when the Holy Spirit interrupted me: *Love keeps no record of wrongs.*

I've heard this verse many times. It's often quoted during weddings since it is part of the well-known chapter about love in 1 Corinthians. But on this night, I wasn't expecting God to drop those words into my heart. They rippled through my mind, disrupting my internal dialogue of disappointments.

You forgive others. You move on when others have wronged you. You give grace and you are patient when everyone else has hard moments. Yet you have no grace for yourself. You keep an endless record of all your wrongs. Becky, I've called you to love others as you love yourself. But you haven't been very kind to yourself lately. God's words to me were like medicine for my aching heart.

Sometimes it's easier to love others than to love ourselves. Isn't it, Momma? Sometimes, we speak kindly to everyone but ourselves. Don't we, Momma? But, my friend, the Lord is clear in His Word when He says, "I will forgive their wrongdoing, and I will never again remember their sins" (Hebrews 8:12, csb). When we confess the sin in our hearts to the Lord, when we ask Him to help us, when we tell Him that how we feel or what we feel has separated us from Him, He removes the shame and the weight and never again remembers our wrongs. And neither should we. Momma, the list of your wonderful accomplishments is so much longer than all the moments where you may feel you missed it. That is a list worth keeping.

Tonight we pray for the momma *who can be so hard on herself. Lord, she tries to be patient and kind and always there for her family. She puts everyone else first over and over, and yet at the end of the day, she often replays her worst moments rather than her best. She thinks about what she believes she did wrong and how she let others down. Tonight, Lord, please wrap Your arms around this momma. Help her hear Your voice listing all the reasons she is exactly the momma her family needs. You are proud of her. Help her believe it.*

We ask in Jesus's name, amen.

Lord, help me see that I am worthy of kindness, too, as I tell myself:

_____

_____

_____

_____

who doesn't know
what she feels

*The steadfast love of the L*ORD* never ceases; his mercies never come to an end;*
they are new every morning; great is your faithfulness.

LAMENTATIONS 3:22-23, ESV

WHEN MARK AND I HAD LITTLE ONES, our house was way out on the northwest edge of Oklahoma City. A small four-lane highway—two lanes coming in and out of town—took us from the city to our home. One morning close to Christmas, I had gone into town to shop at the grocery store. Afterward, I headed west and pulled up to the last stop sign before the road turned into the highway that would take me all the way home. A big flatbed semitrailer filled with Christmas trees was stopped just in front of me. The wonderful piney aroma filled my car, and I smiled as I remembered my favorite Christmas memories. But did I mention I was in a hurry?

I quickly moved to the other lane, only to realize that I was now behind another truck. This one was filled with cattle going to the stockyards. It was stinky and blew stuff on my windshield. Both trucks going west on the same road at the same speed were slowing down my drive home. But I had a choice. I could drive in the Christmas tree lane and inhale a refreshing, woodsy scent, or I could drive in the cattle car lane with the barnyard smell of livestock. There was no passing both trucks. The truth is, no matter the lane I chose to drive in, my experience down the highway that day was impacted by both of them.

Momma, isn't that what life is like sometimes? As we travel through life, we experience a little bit of both. The "aroma" of our day is mixed up as we experience joy and sorrow, happiness and grief, and pleasant memories with current pain. What will we focus on? What lane do we want to align with as we journey forward?

The Lord understands it all. He is with you through every moment of every hard day and every hard night. You can trust in Him. As the Scripture says, "the steadfast love of the LORD never ceases; his mercies never come to an end." Even when you don't know what you feel, let's ask the Lord to help us follow His goodness.

Tonight we pray for the momma *who doesn't really know what she feels. She has been through so much. There are things going on outside of her home, but there is so much happening within her family as well. She is grateful, but she is walking the line between hope and discouragement, joy and pain, peace and frustration. Tonight we ask You to settle her heart. Bring days of peace with the promise of hope. When the sun comes up tomorrow, please give her fresh joy and assurance that it's going to be okay. Help her believe it.*

We ask in Jesus's name, amen.

Father, please help me sort through this mix of emotions tonight so that I may see your new mercies tomorrow:

whose thoughts are racing into tomorrow

We know that in all things God works for the good of those who love him, who have been called according to his purpose.

ROMANS 8:28

MARK AND I WERE WATCHING a presidential address on television. Government officials were announcing a stay-at-home order. Do you remember where you were in March 2020?

In that moment, I started thinking about what I had learned about the Spanish flu from books and movies. I was afraid the world was heading into a similar devastating event. I heard discussions about how people in my age bracket were the ones most likely to have severe consequences from this horrible virus. My thoughts began racing to tomorrow.

"How will we survive this?" I asked Mark, and we made a plan.

It was simple. Our plan was to stay alive. We would sacrifice in the present so we could have a future with our children and family. We stayed home, and we avoided crowded places. We sat out family events. Mark was able to work from home, which was an amazing blessing. We ordered our groceries in and had them left on the black bench on our porch. We just kept saying, "One year for twenty more."

We stayed as vigilant as possible, but at night my thoughts would often race into every tomorrow. Why wasn't this going away? Would it ever end? We wanted our lives back, and we missed the ease of spending time with our children and grandchildren.

Momma, when difficult and unusual circumstances break in on your normal life, it is easy to look to tomorrow with fear. It can be overwhelming to not know how to process new experiences and uncertain times. The Lord knew days like these would come. We haven't been promised an easy answer or an easy life, but God has promised this: "We know that in all things God works for the good of those who love him, who have been called according to his purpose." As we pray tonight, let's keep our thoughts on the One who is present in every tomorrow and who holds us today.

Tonight we pray for the momma *whose thoughts are racing into tomorrow. Lord, no matter how hard she tries to stay in the moment, she can't help but think about the days to come. She thinks of all the different ways things could turn out and worries about each one. Lord, Your Word reminds us that tomorrow will worry about itself. Help this momma catch her racing thoughts and hand them over to You. Help her focus on what You say is true. You are with her. You are loving. You will work it all out for the good of those who love You . . . and that includes her. Give her rest. Cover her with Your peace.*

We ask in Jesus's name, amen.

Lord, please show me where You are in this situation:

who is juggling all the plates

Seek first the kingdom of God and His righteousness, and all these things will be added unto you. Therefore do not worry about tomorrow, for tomorrow will worry about itself.

MATTHEW 6:33-34, BSB

I CLOSED THE LIBRARY BOOK and placed it next to my seven-year-old Jaxton's bed. I prayed for him and gave him one last big hug before I turned out the light and closed the door behind me. I had enjoyed spending this time with him, but at the very same moment, I wondered whether I had spent enough time that day with my other two children. I thought about how I hadn't had a proper conversation with my husband in what felt like a week. I recalled all the work I needed to get done before I turned out my own light for the night.

Truthfully, I'm rarely the momma who reads her kids books before they go to sleep. With two in middle school, it's not often that anyone even wants me to read them a bedtime story anymore. This season is full of practices and ball games in the evenings. I dart from one moment to another, handling one crisis after another, dealing with one more unforeseen situation after another.

I love this life God has given me, but I'm forever juggling the plates—each representing something or someone I've been entrusted with. I'm often so focused on not letting any of them fall that I sacrifice my own peace of mind. I sacrifice my own rest. I let my own heart break to bits with worry and guilt in order to protect each precious plate from peril.

Do you relate? In moments like these I need Jesus to speak directly to my heart. I long to hear Him speak gentle words of grace, like these: *My love is enough. My hope is enough. My peace and my presence are enough. I keep the world spinning, and I hold everything in my hands. As you run from need to need, remember that you're not God . . . I am. So ask Me for help because I'll give it. Ask Me to intervene because I will. Allow My strength to move through you. That's the only way juggling plates don't fall.*

Tonight, Momma, let's lean into the truth that God will help you with each task in front of you. When you seek Him, He will provide all that you need to face whatever may come: "Seek first the kingdom of God and His righteousness, and all these things will be added unto you. Therefore do not worry about tomorrow, for tomorrow will worry about itself." Tomorrow as you move from need to need, person to person, task to task, ask God to help you with each one as it comes. Stay focused, not just on what is right in front of you, but on *who* is with you as you get it all done.

Tonight we pray for the momma *who is juggling all the plates. Lord, she takes care of so much. Whether she's focused on her children, her spouse, her job, or maybe her health or other issues, she keeps going every day, all day until she collapses into bed at night. Then she dreams of what she left unfinished as she waits for the juggling to begin again in the morning. There always seems to be more to do. Tonight, Lord, we ask that You grant this momma peace and rest so she wakes strengthened to face tomorrow. Help her to be kind to herself. Help her see You helping her with what must be done.*

We ask in Jesus's name, amen.

Father, remind me that You
have a firm grip on me and all these plates:

_____

_____

_____

who needs to know it's going to be okay

Then the woman said to Elijah, "Now I know that you are a man of God and that the word of the LORD from your mouth is the truth."

1 KINGS 17:24

ONE SUNNY AFTERNOON IN LOS ANGELES, I sat in my office and looked out the window just as the mail truck pulled to a stop at the end of our quiet cul-de-sac. The world looked bright in a land known for possibilities, but a dark cloud of anxiety hung over my head. When God called Jared and me to California, He didn't tell us how He intended to finance our missionary journey. We stepped out in faith, trusting Him to provide, and He met us each step of the way. But it was a season that continually tested our faith.

On that afternoon, as I watched the mail carrier open our box, I wasn't sure how we were going to pay our rent. Money was coming, but it would arrive in our bank account well past the due date of some very important bills. I thought back to stories my momma had told me about finding money on the ground when she needed it most and receiving unexpected checks in the mail at just the right moment.

So as I watched the mail truck pull away, I hummed a little song to myself and whispered a prayer to the Lord, "Believing for checks in the mail . . . checks in the mail. . . . You can do all things, Lord. Thank You for checks in the mail." And wouldn't you know that tucked inside that ordinary stack of bills, coupon mailers, and advertisements was an unexpected envelope that surprised Jared and me in the best way.

It was the check that wasn't supposed to arrive until the next month. It had come three weeks early! In that moment, God reminded us again that it was all going to be okay.

Have you ever experienced a time when you needed God to show up for you again? Perhaps He made a way before, but you needed to know once more that it was going to be okay.

Remember the story of Elijah and the widow living in Zarephath? When the woman gave Elijah some of the last of her food, God provided miraculously for her, her son, and the prophet throughout the drought. But sometime later, her son became very ill and died.

In her grief, the woman demanded of Elijah: "What do you have against me, man of God? Did you come to remind me of my sin and kill my son?" (1 Kings 17:18). This boy was dearly loved by his mother, who had lost so much. She had lived through the trauma of believing their food would run out. She had seen God come through in the past, but the loss of her son was an unspeakable tragedy.

Elijah, too, was filled with sorrow and questions, but he didn't despair. Instead, he took the boy in his arms and withdrew to pray for him, crying out:

> "Lord my God, let this boy's life return to him!" The Lord heard Elijah's cry, and the boy's life returned to him, and he lived. Elijah picked up the child and carried him down from the room into the house. He gave him to his mother and said, "Look, your son is alive!"
>
> I KINGS 17:21-23

Momma, just like the widow, you may have noticed that one thing rises to the surface every time you pray. You have seen God move in miraculous ways in the past, even if you didn't recognize those moments as miracles. You saw Him provide, bring peace, and give you strength. He has met your needs again and again, but perhaps you are facing another impossible situation. You need to know that God will make a way and it will all turn out okay. Tonight we join our cries with yours, saying "Lord my God, step into this situation and let life return."

Tonight we pray for the momma *who needs to know it's all going to be okay. Lord, she has so many areas where she needs You to intervene, but one particular thing often comes to the surface of her heart, causing her to question if it really is going to be all right. Tonight we ask You to remind her that You always work everything out for her good . . . just because You love her. Quiet every lie that causes her to question Your goodness. Help her believe it's going to be okay. Give her peace.*

We ask in Jesus's name, amen.

Jesus, thank You for being my ever-present help.
Tonight please show me how this one thing will be okay:

who is doing better than she thinks

Jesus grew in wisdom and stature,
and in favor with God and man.

LUKE 2:52

"Do you want mac and cheese for lunch, Becky?"

I already knew the answer because it was her favorite lunch after kindergarten every day. I put the pan on the stove to boil the water, and we both began the ten-minute wait. Often I would peel a fresh apple and cut it up into slices while waiting for the water to boil. Sometimes we used the few minutes to catch up on the latest kindergarten news, such as the alphabet letter of the week and the fun adventures on the playground that morning.

The routine of the everyday did not feel special at the time. The same lunch, same apple, same laughter, and small talk did not feel very important. But what I didn't realize then was that I was stitching together the garment of her childhood. Stitch by stitch, lunch by lunch, I was weaving the story that Becky would remember when she had her own children. It didn't have to be exciting or fancy or special; it just had to be consistent and loving and purposeful. I did not know this then. It just looked like a pan of water, an apple peeler, and a seat at the oak table by the patio door. But it was love on display, and I was doing better than I thought I was.

Momma, what is it that you are doing every day that seems so simple yet, with the magnifier of time, will have such profound effects on your children's hearts? It isn't always the trips to Disneyland they will remember. It is often the routine of the ordinary that becomes the background song of their hearts in their adult years.

When our Lord was with His disciples, He taught them as much as He could every day. He taught them in word and by example. He taught them by sending them out on assignment and then reviewing the assignment when they returned. He shared meals, festivals, and celebrations like the wedding at Cana with them. He lived a life consistent with who He was and what His mission was.

That's what we do as mommas. We encourage, teach by example, and review the assignments we give our children. We model the life of Christ as we do these daily tasks, and in so doing, we teach our children how to live godly lives and help them to grow in stature and in favor with God and man. Tonight be reminded that you are doing better than you think.

Tonight we pray for the momma *who is doing so much better than she thinks. Lord, she pours out her love and yet often wonders if it's enough. Tonight we ask that You'd lean in and remind her how You see her. She is the momma You chose for this job. You know that as she clings to You, the two of you can face anything. You are so proud of her, and You see how hard she tries. Help her feel Your love tonight. Bless her and give her peace.*

We ask in Jesus's name, amen.

Jesus, I trust You to give me the strength and wisdom tomorrow to tackle these tasks:

who is in pain

As they went, they were cleansed.

LUKE 17:14

IT WAS LATE AT NIGHT, and the pain was unrelenting. I couldn't catch my breath, it hurt so much. I had been diagnosed with a large kidney stone the previous week. The day before, my doctor had tried to break it up with a procedure called a lithotripsy, which uses shock waves to break the stone into smaller pieces. Unfortunately, my pieces were still too big to be expelled, and now they were stuck. This resulted in excruciating pain and a fast trip to the emergency room. I was sick for the next month as doctors inserted stents and performed another lithotripsy. I felt like I was caught in an endless cycle of treatment.

I needed the Lord to step in and heal me. I was desperate for His healing touch. I learned in that season that the Lord will walk beside you through every physical trial. I did not receive instant healing, but I did have an excellent urologist, a compassionate team of doctors and nurses, and a supportive family. My employer even held my job open until I could return.

In the Gospel of Luke, we read about ten men who no doubt suffered terrible pain as well.

Now on his way to Jerusalem, Jesus traveled along the border between Samaria and Galilee. As he was going into a village, ten men who had leprosy met him. They stood at a distance and called out in a loud voice, "Jesus, Master, have pity on us!" When he saw them, he said, "Go, show yourselves to the priests."

LUKE 17:11-14

I love how Jesus healed people in so many different ways. He healed some with a command or a touch of His hand. He healed a blind man using mud and instructions to go wash in a certain pool. But these men? He gave them directions to go show themselves to the priest, which is what lepers were required to do if they had been healed. Scripture tells us that "as they went, they were cleansed."

Their healing came during the journey. Momma, if you're in a place where you, too, are crying out, "Master, have pity on me!"

trust this: The Lord sees you and hears you, and He has a plan for your healing. As you walk with Him, may He touch your ailment, speak restoration to your body, and give you instructions on your specific path to healing.

Tonight we pray for the momma *who is hurting. Lord, the pain might be physical or emotional. No matter the cause, she is suffering tonight, and she needs You to bring healing as only You can. Lord, we ask for a miracle. We ask You to remove what's causing her to ache tonight. Your Son suffered on the cross so she could be whole. Tonight we believe for Jesus's sacrifice to bring the healing she needs in her mind, body, and spirit. Bless this momma with rest and peace.*

We ask in Jesus's name, amen.

Jesus, sometimes this pain feels like too much to bear.
I ask for Your comfort and healing touch for . . .

_____

_____

_____

_____

_____

who is doing her best

Come to me, all you who are weary and burdened,
and I will give you rest.

MATTHEW 11:28

WHEN MY HUSBAND, Mark, went into full-time ministry, we had just purchased the small boutique T-shirt company Becky told you about earlier. As part of the transaction, we received some T-shirt designs, a little inventory, and a list of prospective buyers and exhibits.

I have always loved being an entrepreneur, so I was not daunted by the prospect of building this small business into something that could support our family during our major life transition. But I think I underestimated the demands of this new endeavor.

We sold most of our shirts at craft shows and conventions.

Back then, online sales didn't exist, so if people wanted a unique shirt, they had to find us in a field, a building at a fairground, or an exhibit hall. It was fun to have happy customers who were excited to see us and our displays.

The shirts were popular, but the process of setting up, selling, and breaking down our booth at these shows landed squarely on my shoulders. These events typically took place on the weekends when my husband would be in the pulpit. I was doing my best to support his career change and our new ministry while creating enough income for our little family to survive. It was a lot.

I especially remember one night when I was driving back to southern Oklahoma from Arkansas. Not only was it dark and rainy, but also I was tired from three days of sitting in the field at a fall festival. I just wished I were home and could rest. That night—and many other nights if I am being honest—the load felt very heavy. But as I look back, I recognize that the Lord was with me and helped me through that difficult season.

The apostle Matthew recorded this invitation from Jesus: "Come to me, all you who are weary and burdened, and I will give you rest." Momma, when the world seems too heavy to bear, we must remember He has given us this invitation of rest.

The Lord is right beside you, just as He was right beside me on the rainy highway in the middle of the night. He knows how hard you are trying, and He will help you carry the load. But you cannot forget to come to Him.

Whether your children are still at home or you're an empty nester caring for your aging parents, whether you're a businesswoman running your own schedule or employed in a profession that demands much of your time, whether you're loving your current season of life or just so ready for the next, being a momma while being everything else can feel like an incredible load.

If no one has told you, hear me say this: The Lord knows you're doing your best, and He is proud of you. Go to Him tonight in prayer and let Him give you the gift of rest.

Tonight we pray for the momma *who is doing her best. Lord, no matter what gets thrown her way, she keeps doing all she can to care for her children and manage all her other responsibilities. Sometimes the load feels heavy, sometimes very heavy. Today may have been one of those days. Lord, help her tonight. Please bring peace, comfort, and rest.*

We ask in Jesus's name, amen.

Lord, I trust You to carry these burdens,
which I lay down before You now:

who needs a win

I cried unto the LORD with my voice, and
he heard me out of his holy hill.

PSALM 3:4, KJV

"WHAT DO THEY DO WITH ALL THE RED CARPET when the Oscars are over?" I asked my local friend as we walked down Hollywood Boulevard the night before the awards ceremony. The street was packed with tourists and contractors setting up for the next day. Just twenty-four hours later, television crews and celebrities alike would walk the very same street where I now stood.

"I'm not sure," my friend replied.

I was visiting California for a ministry opportunity and to spend time with a new friend. We had a few moments to spare, and she asked what I wanted to do. On my first trip to Los Angeles, all I could think to reply was, "Maybe we could see the Hollywood Walk of Fame." I had no idea that the Oscars would be held there the next day or how much chaos surrounded that portion of an already busy city.

A man laying carpet on the other side of a security fence overheard our conversation. "We get rid of it," he answered. "All of this will be replaced next year." Coming from a small town in Oklahoma, the thought of all that waste seemed inconceivable. I'm sure my face showed it. But then the man did something remarkable.

This guy who looked like he was in charge but was dressed like one of the team picked up his tool, cut a strip from the edge of the carpet, and passed it to me through the fence.

I had no idea that just eighteen months later, my family and I would be living thirty miles from that street or that three years later nearly to the day I'd be invited to walk a red-carpet event at the Chinese Theatre on the same street.

In some seasons of motherhood, we may feel like we've missed our greatest opportunities and our best days are behind us. We think, *Now I'm just a mom, and nothing exciting will ever happen for me again.* But, Momma, God has a perfect plan for you. You may feel like you are on the outside looking at exciting and fun events on the other side of a fence. But there is an open door for you in the Lord's timing. Your dreams are not dead, even if they feel dormant.

The Lord has so many unique gifts and experiences for you in the future that you have no idea about in this moment. Just trust

Him to bring it all to pass. Ask Him, and He will hear your heart: "I cried unto the LORD with my voice, and he heard me out of his holy hill." You will soon realize the purpose of what He is placing into your hands today. Breakthrough is coming, friend. We are believing with you.

Tonight we pray for the momma *who needs a win. Lord, she is exhausted. All the stress, disappointment, and opportunities that have fallen through have made her feel like even hoping for a breakthrough . . . is hopeless. Lord, You see this momma. You see the other side of this mountain that she has named defeat. You know that the two of you will make it to the other side together. We ask that You'd pour fresh hope into her heart. Give her faith to believe in what You are about to do. She's about to experience a breakthrough. Help her see it!*

We ask in Jesus's name, amen.

Father, I ask You to give me fresh hope when it comes to . . .

Index

About the Authors

Becky Thompson is a *USA Today* bestselling author and the founder of the Midnight Mom Devotional online community, a ministry gathering millions of women in nightly prayer. Her ministry focuses on restoring peace to the anxious woman's heart, inviting women into an encounter with God's presence, and teaching women about the life-changing power of prayer. Through her books and dynamic online resources and courses, Becky connects women to the hope found in Jesus alone. Before founding the Midnight Mom Devotional community, Becky earned a bachelor of science in biblical studies from Southwestern Christian University in Bethany, Oklahoma. She graduated summa cum laude.

Becky's books include *Hope Unfolding, Love Unending, Truth Unchanging, My Real Story, Peace, God So Close, Midnight Dad Devotional,* and *Midnight Mom Devotional,* which has sold over one hundred thousand copies. Becky has been a guest on many television, radio, and online programs, including *Focus on the Family, Family Talk with Dr. James Dobson, FamilyLife Today,* and the Billy

Graham Evangelistic Association podcast *GPS: God, People, Stories.* She has been a guest contributor for various online and print magazines, including Crosswalk.com, Fox News, *HomeLife, Mature Living,* and *Relevant.*

Becky resides in northwest Oklahoma with her husband, Jared, and their three children.

Susan K. Pitts is coauthor of the *USA Today* bestselling *Midnight Mom Devotional,* which has sold over one hundred thousand copies. She serves alongside her daughter Becky as the codirector and prayer team leader of the Midnight Mom Devotional online community, a ministry dedicated to leading millions of moms in nightly prayer. Her ministry focus is praying with mommas of all ages and walks of life and leading them to the heart of the Father. She identifies the heartfelt needs of these women and speaks through prayer into those difficult places. Before helping lead the Midnight Mom Devotional community, Susan served for fourteen years as a copastor with her husband, Mark. She earned a bachelor of arts degree from Oral Roberts University.

Susan has written articles for magazines, including *HomeLife, Mature Living,* and *Relevant.* She is active on Facebook and Instagram and has been a guest on numerous radio, television, and online programs, including *FamilyLife Today* and the Billy Graham Evangelistic Association podcast *GPS: God, People, Stories.*

Susan resides in northwest Oklahoma with her husband. They have two adult daughters and three grandchildren. Susan loves to have friends and family over for a home-cooked dinner and lots of laughter. Her favorite room is the dining room, where everyone gathers around the big Mediterranean table, a family heirloom. She is still trying to keep her New England garden alive in the red dirt of Oklahoma.

JOIN THE NIGHTLY GLOBAL PRAYER MOVEMENT
with Mommas Just Like You

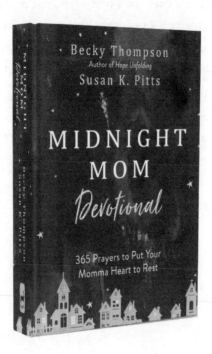

The end of the day can bring so many feelings to the surface of a momma's heart. Pray alongside a community of women who feel just like you do.